BLOCKBUSTERS

ALSO BY GARY S. LYNN

Breaking Through Bureaucracy (with Norman Lynn)
From Concept to Market

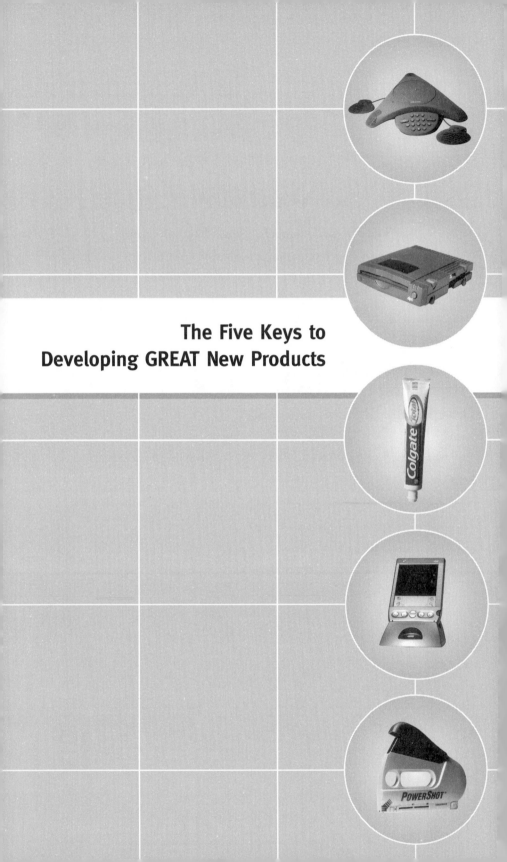

The Five Keys to
Developing GREAT New Products

BLOCKBUSTERS

ary S. Lynn, Ph.D., and Richard R. Reilly, Ph.D.

HarperBusiness
An Imprint of HarperCollins*Publishers*

HarperCollins books may be purchased for educational, business, or sales promotional use. For information please write: Special Markets Department, HarperCollins Publishers Inc., 10 East 53rd Street, New York, NY 10022.

FIRST EDITION

Designed by Kris Tobiassen

Library of Congress Cataloging-in-Publication Data

Lynn, Gary S.
 Blockbusters : the five keys to developing great new products /
 by Gary S. Lynn and Richard R. Reilly.
   p. cm.
 Includes bibliographical references and index.
 ISBN 0-06-008473-1
 1. New products. I. Reilly, Richard R. II. Title.
 HF5415.153 .L95   2002
 658.5'75—dc21   2002068694

02 03 04 05 06 ❖/RRD 10 9 8 7 6 5 4 3 2 1

We would like to dedicate this book to our wives, Nancy and Laura, for all their love, help, and support.

CONTENTS

ACKNOWLEDGMENTS

This book was truly a labor of love. And like love, it has gone through various stages: dating and not knowing where it would wind up; realizing that this was truly something special; deciding that we wanted to make it work and sacrificing to do so. But our efforts were eased by the support of others who also believed in this book and pitched in to help us produce a work we can be proud of.

We are grateful to the Stevens Institute of Technology, and especially to our Dean, Jerry Hultin, former Dean, James Tietjen, and the President of Stevens, Harold Raveche, who have helped us to pursue this research in the context of Technogenesis at Stevens. And to Donald Merino at Stevens for his undying support and belief in this project from the very beginning. Also to the students in the Stevens Executive Masters of Technology Management Program. They have challenged us to dig deeper and find answers to their probing questions concerning innovation as part of courses we teach on new product development and teamwork. The research upon which this book is based benefited greatly from their input.

Several funding agencies provided generous support for this research including the Center of Innovation Management Studies, Institute for the Study of Business Markets, Marketing Science Institute, Stevens Alliance of Technology Management, and the Stevens Center of Technology Management Research at Stevens.

This book is based on quantitative as well as qualitative research. The following people shared information and helped us to better understand the intricacies of many of the stories detailed in the pages of this book: William Armistead, Robert Auchinleck, Randy Battat, Jim Bausch, Jim Bean, Forest Behm, Bob Belleville, Ed Birss, Morry Blumenfeld, Mike Boich, Tom Bonnie, Bob Bowden, Bobby Bowen, Dave Bradley, Tom Buiocchi, Jim Caile, Jim Carlson, Burnum Casterline, Dave Charlton, Arthur Chen, Deme Clainos, Jacques Clay, Ed Colby, Mike Connor, Marty Cooper, John Couch, Alice Crowder, Allen Dawson, Max Downham, Donna Dubinsky, Larry Duffy, David Duke, Richard Dulude, William Dumbaugh, Marcel Durot, Lonnie Edelheit, Kim Edwards, Lew Eggebrecht, Bob Ellinghausen, Chris Espinosa, Noel Fallwell, George Fisher, Bruce Foster, Chris Franklin, Bob Ganger, Jack Germain, Arthur Glenn, Jim Groff, Dick Grote, Jack Haber, Martin Haberli, Dick Hackborn, Rob Haitani, Mel Hallerman, Pat Harrington, Eric Harslem, John Henkes, Andy Hertzfeld, Betsy Hill, Brian Hinman, Barry Homler, Wil Houde, Amory Houghton Jr., John Hutchins, Brian Jaquet, Dave Jones, Mike Kane, Guy Kawasaki, Stuart Kaye, Larry Kelly, Allison Klimerman, Steve Koch, Theodore Kozlowski, George Krieger, Tom Lambert, Rick Leavitt, Doug LeGrande, Daniel Lewin, Don Linder, Bill Lowe, Charles Lucy, Thomas MacAvoy, Joseph McCann, Webb McKinney, Jeannette Mahr, John Mailhot, Joel Marks, Mike Marks, Jim Martz, Susan Marvin, Robert Maurer, Robert Mazur, Ike Mediate, Ron Mehaffey, Jim Michalak, Tim Mikkelsen, Carol Mills, John Mitchell,

Joseph Morone, Annette Mullendore, John Mullendore, Albert Nagele, Rick Nelson, Alan Nonnenberg, David O'Connor, Ken Okin, Rich Page, Peter (Ted) Pashler, Mike Perkins, Gary Pitt, Taylor Pohlman, John Price, William Prindle, Jef Raskin, Rowland ("Red") Redington, Charles Reed, Walt Robb, Jeff Rodman, Larry Rojas, Wayne Rosing, Wendell Sander, Craig Sanford, Joe Sarubbi, Steve Savitz, Ron Schilling, James Schlatter, Dan Searle, Robert Shapiro, Craig Short, Barry Smith, Gail Smith, Laddy Stahl, Edward Staiano, Larry Stewart, Kent Stockwell, Srinivas Sukumar, Bill Sydnes, Dennis Taets, Dan Terpack, John Terry, John Trani, Karl Ulrich, Nathan Ulrich, Alan Vandemoere, William Weiz, Jim White, Jan Winston, George Wise, Phil Worley, Steve Wozniak, Barry Yarkoni, Andrew Zaremba, and Jesse Zuckor. This book would not have been possible without their generous assistance, for which we are most grateful.

We tried to follow our own advice and use the practices outlined in this book. To that end, we sent out very early drafts of this work to subject matter experts. Our thanks to them not only for providing valuable insights but also for doing it in a time frame that surprised everyone: Donald Abraham, Ali Akgün, Greg Alt, William Ausura, Barry Bayus, John Bers, Robert Brentin, Roger Calantone, Gina Colarelli O'Connor, Charlotte Collister, Mike Compeau, Tony Di Benedetto, Peter Dominick, Nancy Dreicer, Larry Gastwirt, Reid Hannon, Tina Kampman, Len Kistner, Peter Koen, George Krieger, Dan Krupka, Adrian Leblanc, Norman Lynn, Karen Merson, Jakki Mohr, Parry Norling, Rich Notargiacomo, Ralph Oliva, Mickey Rosenau, Robert Rothberg, Steve Savitz, Steven Schnaars, Jag Sheth, Fred Shultz, Stanley Slater, Deepak Sukh, Jim Tietjen, Paul Veenema, Joel West, and Brian Yeager.

One of our goals in this book was to make it fun to read. Several individuals provided artwork that is shown in the book allowing the stories to come to life: Roderick Brownfield, Kristine Gable, Lolita Hostetler, Brian Jaquet, George Krieger, Rick Leavitt, Joel Marks, Mike Marks, Holly McDermott, Joel Scharf, and Steven Weyhrich.

We also would like to thank *BusinessWeek* for their series of articles on new products including their "Best Products," "Annual Design Awards," "The Best Product Designs of the Year," and "A Decade of Design"; *Design News* for their "Best Products" articles; *Newsweek* for its Editors Choice Awards; and *Popular Mechanics* and *PC World*, who have given awards for "best" products. These articles helped us to identify some of the products highlighted in the chapters that follow.

All the folks at HarperCollins have been a pleasure to work with. They were responsive and understanding: especially our publisher, Carie Freimuth; associate publisher, Mary Ellen Curley; head of marketing, Lisa Berkowitz; and design director, Lucy Albanese.

We are thankful for having Rafe Sagalyn as our agent; he talked us through many situations and kept us on the right path. We would also like to thank Lorraine Dusky, our editor, collaborator, and friend for helping us to flesh out the complex details of the cases, and for structuring the book in an approachable and accessible manner.

Gary would like to thank his wife, Nancy who provided the initial inspiration that culminated in this book, and to Zachary and Ashley Rose, his two blockbusters. Dick would like to thank Laura for all her support and help.

In writing this book, we tried to implement our five blockbuster practices. Although we don't know yet the impact our efforts will have, we can say that, like most new products, this book experienced many difficulties and obstacles along the way. But if you diligently apply the five practices, regardless of the outcome, you, like us, will get better performance from your team and have a better time in the process.

PREFACE

All companies no matter what size or in what industry need to generate innovative new products and services if they are to win. Increased competition, both domestic and global, the rapid pace of new technology, and changing customer demands have created a marketplace that is more competitive than ever before. One innovative product can alter the future of a single company and lead to entirely new families of products, and may even usher in a whole new industry.

But creating innovative products and services can be like going down a road with seemingly insurmountable challenges, rocks and ruts the whole way. For one new product to be a success in the marketplace, it takes approximately 3,000 raw ideas, 300 patent disclosures, 125 small projects, nine early developmental programs—four that continue to major development, and just under two that are actually launched into the market.[1] One recent study found that newly launched industrial products failed 33 percent of the time; new consumer packaged goods fail to live up to management's expectations 80 percent of the time.[2]

Examples of costly failures are legion. In today's dollars, Federal Express lost $294 million on Zap Mail. NeXt lost $250 million on its computer workstation. GM lost $420 million on the Wankel Rotary Engine. DuPont lost over $1 billion on Corfam. Ford lost over $2 billion on the Edsel. Polaroid wrote off $197 million in inventory alone for "Polarvision" instant movies. Xerox invented the personal computer ahead of Apple but failed to commercialize it successfully. Motorola invested over a decade and more than $360 million in its cellular telephone project before taking a single major order.[3] Corning developed optical fibers only to find itself without a market—it took more than ten years and over $200 million until optical fibers began making money for the company.

Making matters worse, studies have shown that companies are not getting any better at creating new products and services. We believe companies can do better. We believe that the findings we present here will help companies do just that.

BLOCKBUSTERS

① How Blockbusters Happen
Our Research—and Why We Did It

Great companies succeed and endure because they continually produce great products. Companies fail because they have forgotten this simple truth. Manipulating inventory values, accelerating depreciation schedules or moving corporate headquarters offshore does not create value. Even establishing world-class customer service will do little if a company's products* or services are inadequate. To produce real value, companies must develop and launch great, blockbuster products—this is the heart and soul of any successful business. How to do just that is what this book is all about.

How do blockbusters happen? Is there a way to analyze what blockbuster new product development teams do right? And can your teams learn from those extraordinarily successful teams? We have been looking for the answers to these questions for over a decade. In the process, we have investigated the policies and practices of more than seven hundred new product development teams—including

---

* We use the term "products" to encompass both products as well as services.

several who created some of the most successful products ever developed that became household names, such as the Black & Decker Dustbuster, the IBM PC, and Corning optical fibers.

The blockbuster teams whose keys to success we uncovered had enormous impact not only on their companies, but their industries as well. Consider:

Colgate Total toothpaste became the best-selling toothpaste in its first month on the market, knocking Crest from its vaunted position after thirty-five years. Motorola's cellular telephones created a whole new multibillion-dollar division for the company. AT&T's transistor ushered in the computer revolution. The Zip Drive computer storage device saved Iomega from near death in 1994. CAT scanners allowed General Electric to dominate the medical imaging field for two decades. Plain paper photocopying provided Xerox with a platform upon which it created a new industry. The Apple IIe cemented Apple's leadership in computers for *six* years—several lifetimes in the world of high tech—and in the process made personal computers a reality for the home user. The Handspring Visor, a personal digital assistant, captured 25 percent of the U.S. market a mere month after launch. Corning's optical fiber turned the company around from a glass manufacturer to a provider of telecommunications equipment and, along the way, revolutionized long-distance communication.

How did they do it? What were their "secrets"? Did the companies and new product development teams that developed these blockbuster products have anything in common? And if they did, can we generalize from their formula for success so that other companies can follow it when creating new products? The answer, in a nutshell, is *yes*. After analyzing new product development teams from disparate companies big and small that make everything from

Army tanks to chewing gum to computers, and after studying teams that have created blockbusters and those that have developed flops, we believe that we've discovered their "secrets," the five critical practices that blockbuster teams follow and that losers do not.

We have reached our conclusions only after a decade-long journey that began in 1992 when Gary, a former R&D director, launched a study about how new product development teams functioned. In 1996 he accepted a position at the Stevens Institute of Technology, where Dick, an organizational psychologist whose specialty is statistics, was a professor. Within a month, we decided to pool our expertise, and began what would turn out to be a ten-year research study of how highly successful new products are brought to market.

We found that almost no research had been done on the subject of how blockbusters are developed and commercialized. Yes, there were books and articles on incremental innovation, radical innovation, breakthroughs and disruptive innovation, but no one had written about how companies develop and commercialize products that become blockbusters—and compared and contrasted their strategies with those of not-so-successful products, as well as downright failures. Only when you did the two could you accurately determine those factors that are particularly critical for extraordinarily successful new products. We set that as our goal. Thus, ours is the only multiphase, systematic, large-scale study of extraordinarily successful, award-winning—*blockbuster*—successes, as well as not-so-successful teams and outright failures, that anyone has ever done.

As we began collecting data from various new product development teams, we knew we had to find a way to factor out those aspects of team behavior that were merely background "noise" and did not impact outcome, and concentrate on those practices that did. This proved to be one of our toughest challenges.

BENCHMARKING FOR SUCCESS

The first step was to figure out how to design a research protocol that would ferret out truly world-class "best" practices from the moderately successful ones. The technique for doing this is known as *benchmarking*, a system developed at Xerox, where it is defined as "the continuous process of measuring products, services, and practices against the toughest competitors or those companies recognized as industry leaders."[1]

By adopting the best practices that benchmarking identifies, companies can achieve truly phenomenal gains, sometimes as great as 2,000 percent, and in as short a time as eight months.[2] The typical new process adopted in this way reduces cost, cycle time, and error rates by up to 60 percent.[3] With benchmarking, Cadillac reduced customer complaints by 60 percent; Western Electric lowered manufacturing operations inventory by $1 billion,[4] and Fuji Xerox doubled profits in its thirty-two retail outlets in just a year.[5] Not surprisingly, many companies have employed this research technique as the tool of choice for improving operations.

But benchmarking effectively requires knowing what and whom to benchmark. Consider what happened to Lance Armstrong in the 2000 Olympics. As the four-time Tour de France winner, he was the overall favorite, but a simple mistake cost him the gold. He was drafting a pack of riders near the final leg of the race—saving his energy so he could blow past them in the final minutes for victory. When he finally moved to pass, though, Armstrong realized that the group he was drafting was *not in the lead.* The lead pack was so far out in front that he was unable to catch them. Armstrong had to settle for the bronze.

It's the same in industry; to use benchmarking successfully, you need to know who's really out in front, that is, what practices are really world-class, as opposed to those which seem like the best because they belong to the so-called great companies that you happen to have access to. And even if you do have access to such world-class companies, identifying best practices being initiated by their new product development (NPD) teams is tricky. Because of the secretive and proprietary nature of NPD, companies are understandably reluctant to share such information, especially that which they feel gives them a competitive advantage.

Unfortunately, two of the most common approaches to benchmarking—practitioner and academic—can lead to faulty information, and the same sort of mistake in business that Lance Armstrong made at the Olympics.

In the *practitioner* mode, one typically uses a "nearest neighbor" approach—that is, the pool of data is drawn from the most recent and accessible successes. One weakness is obvious: the best practices of your nearest neighbor may not be truly world-class. But there is a deeper flaw. Without a systematic study of failures as well as successes, you might draw the wrong conclusions. Say several successful NPD teams began each morning singing the company song. If you only studied these teams, you might conclude that singing is critical. But suppose teams whose products failed *also* sang every morning. Any conclusion drawn from singing would be meaningless. By studying only successful teams, you fail to eliminate those practices that are immaterial to attaining success. We've seen a great many books that recommend the management equivalent of singing the company song, and we wanted to avoid making the same mistake.

The *academic* approach seems more promising. Researchers gather information on a variety of NPD teams from one or more companies, and they divide the teams into two groups—best and poor—based on how the products eventually fared in the market. This solves the company song problem, but still comes up short. By definition, the "best" teams are the best only among those in the study—and all the companies or products studied might be mediocre. Or the companies might be in a new industry, such as the Internet business sectors, where optimum practices are not as yet refined. Furthermore, a company's reputation may have been built on any number of other factors, such as effective distribution, excellent marketing, or timely acquisitions—it might not have exemplary innovation practices at all. Consequently, the best practices determined by the academic method are again more a function of the sample than of truly outstanding, world-class practices.

As a result of these shortcomings, both methodologies are flawed: the practitioner approach cannot be statistically validated, or its conclusions generalized across companies or industries; the academic model suffers because the NPD teams included may not be first-rate at all, but merely above average. For benchmarking to be truly valuable, the teams observed *must* be world-class, and successes *must* be contrasted with failures. To do that, you would need to study an exorbitantly large sample of NPD teams.

BENCHMARKING THE BEST OF THE BEST

That's where we come in. Together we created a detailed survey or "innovation report card" (see Appendix 1), as we call it, and began collecting data from a wide variety of NPD teams. We asked some companies if we could survey them, and as our research became known, companies invited us to rate their NPD teams. By 1998, our database had grown to approximately 250 teams in different industries, in different locations, and of different sizes. Our survey had gone through several permutations. We had learned how to filter out those factors, such as organizational differences, personality clashes, market quirks, environmental conditions and regulations, funding starts and stops, personnel changes, and management involvement or interference, that did not impact a team's success. During this time, we were conducting classes and workshops for CEOs, corporate vice presidents, and senior managers teaching them how to analyze their own teams and improve their performance. A representative from the Department of Defense (DOD) attended one of our classes, and a few months later, we got a call from the DOD: Would we be interested in evaluating one of their new product development teams?

We were very interested, because the DOD virtually invented the concept of project management in the 1960s to run their huge and complex programs at the National Aeronautics and Space Administration. It coined the term *phase review* and in the 1970s and '80s refined the process to what they call their *milestone process,* which became known in the commercial sector as the *Stage-Gate* * process, or *toll-gate process.* Additionally, DOD project managers go through the most intensive project management training available anywhere in the country.

Our task was to analyze a team at the U.S. Army's Communications-Electronics Command Research Center (CECOM) in Fort Monmouth, New Jersey, a team that had already been recognized as one of the best in the DOD. We were not only to assess what this

---

* The term *Stage-Gate* was coined by Robert Cooper of McMaster University.

team did right, but also to submit recommendations that other DOD teams could follow.

After the team leaders completed our detailed questionnaire, we followed up with in-depth interviews, several of which we videotaped, and wrote our report and recommendations. After we presented our results to CECOM, the DOD expanded our research, and in 1999 we presented our findings to the Office of the Secretary of Defense at the Pentagon. Since that time, we have worked with a variety of branches in the DOD, including the Army Research Laboratory, the Picatinny Arsenal Research Center, NASA, and numerous defense contractors, over a hundred teams in all.

During our work for the DOD, we began to focus on extraordinarily successful new product teams, both in the government as well as in the commercial sector, always with the goal of ferreting out world-class "best practices." We set the bar high: we were looking for those teams that hit the ball out of the park—those who were not only exceedingly successful in terms of return-on-investment, market share, and sales, but also who had won at least one major award for excellence in their company or industry.

OUR RESEARCH PROTOCOL

The most challenging aspect of this research for us was developing a reliable way to measure what new product teams did right and wrong. This took us several years. Gary had started the ball rolling in the early nineties with a series of qualitative in-depth case studies of seventeen NPD teams from seven companies that produced both consumer goods and industrial products. Companies that participated in this initial phase of the study were Apple Computer, Corning,

General Electric, Hewlett-Packard, IBM, Motorola, and the Searle Division of Monsanto, now part of J. W. Childs Equity Partners.

The next step was our joint research of several hundred NPD teams, using our detailed quantitative survey. Some companies that participated in this stage include AT&T, Cisco Systems, Corning, Honeywell/Allied Signal, American Express, Johnson & Johnson, Merck, Nabisco, NOVARTIS, PSE&G, Unilever, teams from the DOD including NASA, and many start-up companies. (We provide a more complete list in appendix 2.)

As our project grew in scope and became more focused over the decade, we continued to refine our measurement methodology. Our initial questionnaire had 66 items on it; that grew to 245. We ended up with hard data on over 700 distinct projects, and complete data on 611 projects. We classified the NPD teams into three groups: *failures* (215), *moderate successes* (296 non–award winners), and *blockbusters* (successful award-winners) (100).

To identify the "best" of the best practices, we then reviewed the projects of the top 100 teams. Those were the teams who had garnered either an award from their own company or one for industry excellence, such as the Secretary of Defense Team Excellence Award or the Supplier of the Year Award, or had been singled out by prestigious national publications such as *BusinessWeek, Design News, Newsweek, PC World,* and *Popular Mechanics.* We screened them again, now selecting only those award winners who scored a "perfect ten" in meeting company goals *and* meeting or exceeding customer expectations, *and* meeting or surpassing profit and sales expectations. Thirty-four teams met all of these criteria.

To validate our findings, we then sought out an additional fifteen teams that met our standards for blockbuster success; they did not complete our quantitative survey, and hence are not included in the database we used for the charts in the book. The remaining fifty-one award-winning teams were deleted from our statistical analysis because they were not blockbusters as we defined them, nor were they moderate successes or failures.

We spent the following two years looking at how these forty-nine blockbuster teams did what they did, analyzing every phase of their development process from concept to launch, and following up in most cases with lengthy personal interviews. We looked at what the individuals on a team did on a day-to-day basis—how well they communicated, how they met deadlines, what impact the deadlines had on the team, how often they held meetings, how those meetings were structured, how well they stayed focused on the product's initial vision, how they tested their new products, how much senior management was involved, how they got funding, and so on.

In the course of our decade-long research we interviewed over four hundred individuals. We ended up with approximately two thousand single-spaced typed pages of notes from our discussions with project leaders, team members, senior executives, and CEOs who were intimately involved in the development and launch of these products. Some individuals were interviewed up to five separate times in order to clarify and verify the facts. These interviews and the quantitative surveys together provided us with a mountain of information. To process all this data, we filtered out those factors that were beyond the control of the team, such as the competitive climate, or the spark of inventive genius that cannot be predicted accurately or systematically managed. We identified, measured, and assessed the five critical practices that blockbuster teams implemented during their new product development. What made the five essential practices so obvious was the level to which they were present on the blockbuster teams, and their relative absence on the moderate successes and failed teams.

THE FIVE CRITICAL PRACTICES

So what were the five "golden rules" of new product development that made the difference? Let's take a look:

Commitment **Not** *Contribution* **of** *Senior Management.* Blockbuster teams had the full cooperation of the highest level of management. Senior managers were either intimately involved with virtually every aspect of the process, or they made it clear that they completely backed the project, and then gave the team the authority it needed to proceed.

Clear and Stable Vision. Blockbuster teams stayed on course by establishing "project pillars" early on—specific, immutable goals for the product that the team *must* deliver.

Improvisation. Blockbuster teams did not follow a structured, linear path to market. Instead they moved "Lickety Stick." That is, they were flexible, trying all kinds of different ideas and iterations in rapid succession (lickety) until they developed a prototype that clicked with their customers (stick).

Information Exchange. Blockbuster teams did not limit their information exchange to formal meetings. They shared knowledge in dozens of small ways—from coffee klatches to video conferencing to streaming in and out of a room covered in Post-it notes to hundreds of emails.

Collaboration Under Pressure. Blockbuster teams focused on goals and objectives as opposed to interpersonal differences. They built coherent teams, yes, but they were not especially concerned about building friendships or even insisting that everyone like each other.

These five practices fit together like interlocking pieces to a puzzle, and it was this "fit" that helped teams create blockbusters. Implementing one or two of the practices is not enough. This is an important finding, because over the past two decades a plethora of books on new product development have come out, each focusing on a single piece of the new product puzzle: some concentrate on teams and teaming, some on the process, some on marketing, some on prototyping, and some on radical, or disruptive, technologies.[6] None of them has put the new product puzzle all together.

We were surprised that some factors we initially thought might have an impact made no difference at all: blockbusters were just as likely to come from small companies as big ones; big teams were just as successful as small ones; the type of new product or service represented was irrelevant. We also discovered that great companies do not necessarily produce blockbuster products, and blockbuster products do not necessarily produce great companies.

WHAT THIS BOOK DOES—AND DOESN'T—DO

We believe that if your team excels at these five practices, its probability of failure is virtually zero. That's our promise, and it's a promise that we have demonstrated statistically. The second bit of good news is that these practices are all within your control. We do not say that you must, for example, launch a product into a market that is not competitive, because you may not have a choice. We do not suggest that your new product must be technologically ten years ahead of the competition because that may be impossible. We do not suggest that your new product has to be ten times better than the competition. We understand that many times you have to play with the cards you are dealt, that you must launch your new product in the world as it is.

The bad news is this is not going to be an easy journey. Your team must implement *all five practices* to succeed. There is no shortcut. If you implement four out of the five practices, your chances of success go down significantly, a topic we take up in detail in the next chapter.

We also want to stress that this book is *not* about incremental innovation, continuous process improvement, or day-to-day innovation. It is about creating a blockbuster new product that knocks your competitor out of the box, sets a new standard for your industry, and possibly creates a new market category. This book is also *not* about disruptive technologies or changing your entire new product development process; nor is it about changing your corporate culture, your incentive system, or your organizational structure. This book is about the five essential practices that can help you launch one—not a family of them, just one—blockbuster product per division.

In the following chapters, we will discuss how these five practices worked for several of the most profitable teams ever assembled, and how they can work for your company. Our goal is to help you establish the kind of superperforming teams that set new standards for your industry. You will learn about some of the best new products ever launched, and the stories of the teams who launched them. You will learn how to implement each of the five practices so that you can develop and launch the kind of innovative products and services your company needs to grow and prosper. In short, you will learn how to create the next blockbuster in your industry.

2

The Five Critical Practices at Work

Putting the Puzzle Together at Iomega

When we began our research project, we figured that we would find several common denominators on the blockbuster teams. What we did not expect was how important it would be that all five practices be done together.

But we found that blockbuster teams did not excel in only two or three of the practices and then flunk the rest; they excelled at *all five* of the practices. When they failed to achieve a high degree of competency in even one practice, their chances of achieving blockbuster success diminished significantly.

Using a statistical technique called *discriminant analysis,* we broke the teams we studied into three groups: failures, moderate successes, and blockbusters. If a team executed the five practices poorly or not at all, its probability of failure was almost 100 percent. If, however, a team excelled at these five practices, its probability of failure was only 2 percent.

Probability of Failure, Success, or Blockbuster
When All Five Practices Are Implemented at the Highest Level

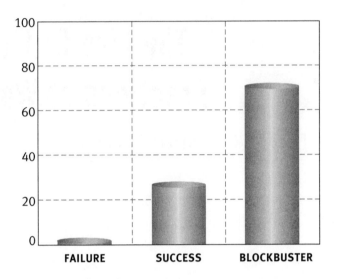

FIGURE 2.1

Discriminant analysis allowed us to determine the probability of a team being in each of three groups when all five practices were performed at the highest level of proficiency. The probability of being a blockbuster if you do all five practices well is 71 percent, and the probability of being a failure is only 2 percent. Although 71 percent does not guarantee a blockbuster, let's put it in context. If you excel at all of the five practices, even if you don't get a blockbuster, your chances of being at least moderately successful are 98 percent.

In the pages to come we will discuss each of the practices in detail and illustrate it with a case study of a blockbuster team. We will also show how you can make each practice part of your new product development program. But before we discuss the specifics of each of the five golden rules of NPD, we want to show how one company implemented all five—sometimes with much caviling and foot-dragging—as team members took part in one of the most successful product launches in recent history.

The company desperately needed a new product. Three years earlier, it had been a flourishing firm in the information technology industry, but aggressive competition and technological advances by others were leaving the company's product line in the dust. Nearly half of its workforce had been laid off. Stock was trading under $2.50 a share, an all-time low; pieces of the company had been sold. Needless to say, an aura of gloom permeated the air from the boardroom to the shop floor.

But just when the company was about to flatline, it engineered a remarkable comeback. A new CEO arrived to perform entrepreneurial CPR, and in little more than a year, the company was *shipping* an innovative new product that took the market by storm. Four months later, the company's stock shot up from just under $7 a share to an after-stock-split equivalent of $112 a share. In the first full year of sales, a million units were shipped.[1] In two years, sales increased from $141 million to *$1.2 billion,* climbing in the next year to $1.7 billion with $115 million in net income.

The company was Iomega. Their blockbuster was the Zip Drive. How was Iomega able to accomplish such a remarkable turnaround? By integrating the five key practices throughout its product development process. Doing so was not a matter of starting with one practice, and then moving methodically through two to five. Each of the practices—senior management involvement, clear and stable vision, improvisation, information exchange, and collaboration under pressure—impacted the others and remained in play throughout the entire development process, from concept to market.

PUTTING THE PUZZLE TOGETHER AT IOMEGA

Iomega was founded in 1980, as a spinoff of a Tucson-based IBM research facility. Its main product line was the Bernoulli Box—a removable, reliable floppy disk drive that could archive and transport large amounts of data. The box was so named because it worked on Bernoulli's principle: as the speed of a moving fluid increases, its pressure decreases. It spun the disk at such a high speed that the disk actually curved *up* to the drive head, as opposed to having the drive head move down to the disk—thereby virtually eliminating the possibility of a disk crash.

The first Bernoulli Box held five megabytes of information on one disk and operated ten times faster than standard floppy disks in copying data. The problem was that at a whopping price of $3,795, the Bernoulli Box was far too expensive for the mass market. Only the government was interested. The U.S. Navy appreciated the Bernoulli Box's ruggedness—it could withstand fourteen-foot swells and indirect artillery hits—but these are hardly the requirements of everyday consumers. Nonetheless, with the technology revolution going into high gear, the company optimistically went public in 1983.

Iomega retooled the Bernoulli Box, and in 1985 a new, improved storage drive for the PC mass market was priced at a more affordable $499, plus $99 for each disk. Iomega enjoyed a short boost in sales. But the Bernoulli Box wasn't out there alone. SyQuest was an aggressive competitor with a better product for storing graphics, making their products more appealing to Macintosh users. Since Macs were the computer of choice for publishing and advertising end users, SyQuest was able to win most of that market handily, a considerable blow to Iomega. The Bernoulli Box, furthermore, was a nightmare to install. You had to be a techie to get through the pages of detailed instructions. The Bernoulli Box was plainly headed for the ash heap of technology.

In 1987, the company posted a $37 million loss. Now located on the outskirts of Salt Lake City, a plant built there that never opened became a $5 million albatross. Half the workforce of approximately seven hundred had been laid off. For the next few years, Iomega lumbered on, producing a number of iterations of the Bernoulli drive, as well as other external storage devices. Revenues actually grew, but R&D ate up a good portion of profits. By late 1993, Iomega was sinking fast. With its stock hovering below $2.50 a share, the board of directors looked for a new CEO to shake things up. They found him in Kim Edwards, a former General Electric executive. Outspoken and energetic, Edwards knew that a new and different kind of product was needed to revive the flagging company. Hear what he had to say about his initial encounter with Iomega's flagship product:

When I interviewed for the presidency of the company, the chairman sent me a Bernoulli Box. I spent five hours trying to set it up. It came in a box that was three feet by three feet by three feet and with an instruction book that says, "Read This First," and three more instruction sheets and manuals—over a hundred pages in all written in lots of jargon on how to install this thing. Then I pull out the Bernoulli Box and find that I'm going to have to open my computer and throw DIP switches. I said to my wife, "I haven't the faintest idea what a DIP switch is and, more important, I never want to learn." So I shove this thing back in the box, and I put it in my closet and I kept it there the whole time I was CEO at Iomega to remind me how bad this thing was from the very, very first impression.

Though he was a marketing and sales executive by experience, Edwards was an engineer by degree. If he couldn't install it, how could the average user?

When Edwards arrived at Iomega on the first workday of 1994, the faltering company had two products under development. Both were pushing the technological envelope, and neither was what customers wanted. One was yet another variation of the existing Bernoulli Box; the other, a hopelessly complicated removable disk drive that even Rube Goldberg, says Edwards, couldn't have conceived. "This baby is ugly," I said, "and we're going to have to give birth to a new baby to succeed."

Never one to mince words, his memo to employees on his first day read in part: "We are not developing new products in an efficient timely manner. In simpler terms, our new products are coming out at a snail's pace when, to be competitive, they need to come out at light speed. I do not want to hear any excuses. . . ." Employees did not appreciate hearing that the products they were working on were dinosaurs. "There was major resistance to what I was suggesting at the beginning," says Edwards. "I remember standing up before the organization at an all-employees meeting and feeling like I was being hit with arrows from all sides."

He insisted that the whole company change direction. Not only were the other projects under development abandoned, but the marketing and corporate positioning—even the Iomega logo—were changed to reflect the new Iomega, the one that projected not only cutting-edge technology, but *friendly* cutting-edge technology. In the world of high tech, this was a new, new thing. People who didn't buy into his vision had two choices, Edwards says: "Get off the train or get thrown off." He did not want to squander dwindling financial resources on anyone not going the same direction he was taking the company. During this shakeout period, nearly a third of the employees were either fired or pressured out, taking the payroll down to around 550 people. It was a nervous time for those who stayed.

Three months later, on April 1, Edwards and the senior R&D director, George Krieger, had a firm idea of what kind of innovative product was required: a new type of storage device, unlike anything currently available—code name: Vitamin C. They developed very specific parameters:

1. It had to store 100 megabytes of data.

2. It didn't have to store data at the speed of light, but it had to be "fast enough."

3. It had to sell for between $200 and $300 for an external drive, less for an internal drive.

4. It had to be ridiculously simple to install.

5. And it had to be ready for the industry's annual trade show, Comdex, that *November.*

It was already April. To do all that, Vitamin C would have to take a giant leap technologically, but Edwards was adamant. He assured the team that he would give them all the support they needed to do what had to be done. The alternative he proposed was bleak: *"No Comdex, no company, no choice."*

The deadline left a mere eight months for product development, less than half the time of previous new projects. The compressed schedule was a key part of demonstrating that the company was a new and different Iomega, Edwards says, one where speedy development was the norm.

He handpicked the team, a dozen or so bright, motivated people, some of whom he had worked with before at other high-tech companies, others who had been at Iomega for years. Edwards cleaned out the old Iomega marketing department, which was made up mostly of engineers with little marketing savvy, and replaced all but a handful of them; but left Krieger alone in R&D. "I remember Edwards telling me in February to fire one person in my department, and I said, 'Fuck no.' I was ready to quit rather than fire this guy." Edwards remembers the guy he wanted fired as a vocal critic of the new direction; Krieger says he was one of his best engineers.

The other engineers who had been with Iomega for years did not take kindly to Edwards, the technological neophyte, telling them they came up short. They were smarting over having to dump two years of their hard work, and there was a lot of grousing at first. Keenly aware of their antagonism, Edwards was reluctant to visit the lab, and he frequently called Krieger to stay informed. Krieger finally told him to go down to the lab and get to know the guys. "It took a while for Edwards to earn their respect" says Krieger. Edwards began dropping in first thing in the morning for coffee with the engineers. "Anywhere from two or three up to twelve people showed up," Edwards says. "Sometimes we met in their offices, sometimes in a small conference room. It was very informal. I met with them every day for months on end." The discussions were daily status updates and valuable information exchanges. Everybody knew what was going on, and what remained to be done. Edwards kept up his frequent visits to the R&D lab, constantly reminding everybody of the vision of the new product, of what it *had to be.*

Edwards kept telling them that they could break the rules to accomplish their mission, but the team did not believe him—until one telling incident. They had wanted a new computer, but not just any computer—a Silicon Graphics (SGI) workstation, a computational graphics workhorse that would speed up design. The trouble was, by the time they added on the necessary software, it would cost around $50,000. In the past, they said, they would have been ridiculed for even asking to spend that kind of money. But much to their surprise, once someone mentioned to Edwards that they wanted the SGI machine, "I told them that I was on my way back to my office, and that if they brought necessary paperwork over in the next hour, I would approve it immediately," he says. "They did and we bought two." It was a turning point. The engineers finally understood that Edwards really was on their team, and would help them do whatever they needed to succeed.

The gravity of Iomega's situation—and Edwards's insistent involvement—eventually won everybody over. "I talked about having a maniacal focus," says Edwards. "This is what we *have* to do, and anything that gets in its way has to be removed." The company mantra became: No Comdex, no company, no choice. Engineering director Dave Jones recalls that one person on his team did not believe Vitamin C could be ready in time. "I had to align him," he dryly comments. Development director and team member Clark Bruderer says, "I remember having my own attitude adjusted, but once I did, it was amazing what we achieved."[2]

The shortened development cycle pushed everyone to deliver at peak performance, and besides, Edwards was their constant coach. "What can we do to get the price down?" he would ask. Or he would remind them that "it has to be fast—but only fast enough." If you really want to maximize performance, you can't tell people what to do, he continues. "You have to help them get there. If you say, 'I'm going to take you out and you're going to run a hundred-yard dash in 9.5 seconds,' you're never going to get there. You have to run alongside and tell them what's necessary to do it." With this kind of coaching, the engineers became determined to prove they were up to the task. If the project failed, it wouldn't be their fault.

"I had guys working for me and in other departments who were busting the rules, trying to figure out better, faster ways to do things," asserts Jones. "One rule was: *Nothing is sacred.* Anything can be questioned if it looks like it's in the way." He adds that "it almost felt like cheating to have the CEO on your team." He says it was like showing up late for team practice but walking in with the coach—only now the whole team was walking in with the coach. It was okay to break some rules when the CEO was on your side. It was that kind of we're-all-in-this-together feeling Edwards eventually got across to his players. And eventually everyone had the fire in the belly. They were going to make this baby work or they were going to go down slugging. If anybody did question what they were doing, team members replied that they had God on their side—Edwards, that is.

Manufacturing engineer Rick Leavitt remembers, "We owned this project, and we just made it happen—we got on planes, we talked to vendors."[3] Long hours became a badge of commitment. Engineer Carl Nicklos recalls how he and coworker Mike Lyon kept coming to work earlier and earlier. "I would show up at five A.M.; then he would show up at four A.M.," Nicklos says. "Finally, I didn't go home one night at all."[4]

After talking with potential customers and analyzing the market, the target selling price for the external drive was confirmed ($199) and the internal drive was developed ($100). The low price was a stickler, and R&D was having a hard time buying into the idea that they could get there. One day Krieger saw a tape rewinder at Wal-Mart for $9.99. He threw it in his shopping cart. "I took the thing home and opened it up and saw that Iomega couldn't have even bought the parts for $9.99, let alone the labor and overhead," he says. "If you dropped the tape rewinder, it fell apart, but you could put it back together in thirty seconds and it worked—it was that simple. I took it in the shop the next day and said, 'This is what we gotta do. Find a way to make our thing simpler and cheaper.' That triggered a whole raft of buying different stuff that had a really low price—electronic gizmos you use around the house, car radios, CD players. We had to think outside the box about how to get the cost down."

During this turbulent time, it was not unusual for the engineers in R&D to make two or three changes *per day* on parts. In all, the team built more than fifty stereo lithography models, plus dozens of rapid-prototype molded urethane models. Says Krieger, "It was like turning a Checker cab into a sports car—you have to start from scratch."

Though all cylinders were firing on the Zip program, conflicts still arose among different functional areas, each with its own agenda. In the old Iomega, marketing got no respect from R&D, and though nearly all the old marketers were gone, the new players hadn't yet earned the confidence of the engineers. And then there was that group of outsiders from the industrial design firm, Fitch Inc., that Edwards brought in early on to help refine the design of the new storage drive.

"The original drive had been designed in-house—it looked like a generic dark gray box," says the Fitch executive who ran the project, Spencer Murrell. "There was a lot of animosity when their design got killed—animosity and skepticism." But everybody had a job to do—it didn't matter if R&D didn't like the outsiders. Fitch talked to people at trade shows, interviewed sales people where the product would be sold, and held two dozen focus groups with both non-techies and professional users from May to October. They showed them possible designs with 3-D models. Using blocks covered with Velcro strips, they had people putting together models of what they thought the design for the new product ought to be. Someone from Iomega's marketing department observed every single focus group through a one-way mirror, and brought back a video to show to engineering.

Yet when the news came back that the top-loading feature (like many portable CD players) was a design glitch, Krieger and Jones wanted to see for themselves. They didn't want to believe their design could be, ah, improved by a bunch of marketing-type nonengineers. So Krieger and Jones went themselves to sit behind the one-way mirror at a couple of focus groups in Cincinnati. They returned to Utah convinced they needed to tweak the design. Within days, R&D turned the unit from a top-loader to a front loader (like a floppy disk drive). After that, when Fitch

The first prototype of the Zip Drive—called Vitamin C. It had a flip-up top that focus group participants saw and disliked.
Photograph by Daria Amato.

told the engineers the design had to be personal, portable, and powerful, they listened. In all, the team built more than fifty prototypes to test a variety of different concepts.

Over the summer of 1994, the team held weekly cross-functional meetings that became informative rather than a finger-pointing exercise. By midsummer, engineering, marketing, sales, advertising, and operations were cooperating like different parts of a well-oiled machine. They had to; Comdex was looming and rapidly approaching. Impromptu discussions, by phone, by the coffeepot, in the hallway, kept everybody in the loop.

Even Fitch was part of the loop. Edwards was on the phone every day with someone from Fitch, and during the later stages of development, so were engineers. The entire Fitch team came from Columbus for monthly meetings, and during the final countdown to Comdex, Fitch had someone stationed full-time at Iomega in Roy, Utah, for an entire month. Along the way, someone from Fitch renamed Vitamin C the Zip Drive, a bit of marketing brilliance that connoted speed, ease of use, and a certain perky user-friendly quality, like a name you would give a puppy. Even the Iomega engineers conceded it was good.

In the end, the design for Zip had only twenty-two molded parts, and more than twenty new patents. It represented a breakthrough technologically, and it came together just days before Comdex opened in Las Vegas the third week of November 1994. The size of a small jewelry box, Zip was royal blue in color, lightweight, easily portable, and it could store a hundred megabytes of data.

Zip was a showstopper. Iomega's Comdex booth was packed and the Zip Drive was the hit of the show. Media coverage and word-of-mouth spread the news. Five weeks later in San Francisco at the Apple trade show, MacWorld, the response was like a feeding frenzy,

Edwards says. "You couldn't move in our booth. People were jammed in there, shoulder to shoulder, wanting to play with it, wanting to buy one. They said, 'If I give you my money now, would you put me on a wait list?' That's how it was for four days in a row. We had reporters and retailers in there watching and saying, 'This is incredible.' "

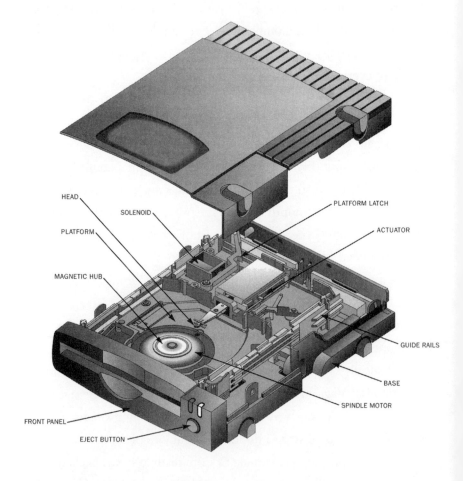

The Zip design was completed using only computer-generated images and drawings. Prototypes were built directly from these computer files. This computer image shows the Zip design with the window that allowed users to see their disk after it had been inserted. Courtesy of Design News, November 6, 1995, Reed Business Information.

The first Zip 100 Drive was a huge hit
at Comdex, and revolutionized
personal data storage.
Photograph by Daria Amato.

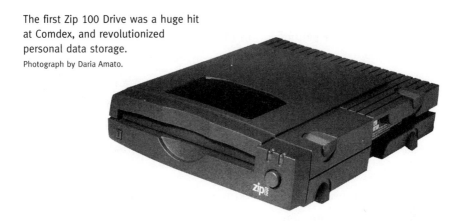

The first Zip Drives were shipped on schedule in March. The whole project from inception to delivery took only eleven months, less than half the development time Iomega had allotted for previous products. The first big sales were to Mac users in advertising and other design fields who created graphics on the computer. The graphic files could be stored on a Zip Drive and sent to the print shop that way. "Everybody was blown away by how well it worked and how easy it was to use," says Tom Dusky, an art director in Detroit. "It was inexpensive and had a good amount of storage. It was half the size of the SyQuest product and weighed about a quarter as much. You could put it in your briefcase." He bought one—and some stock in Iomega—right after he read rave reviews for the Zip in a trade publication.

The initial sales target was 200,000 units for the first twelve months. It sold a million instead. "We all thought that we were dreaming, even thinking that we could ever sell 500,000 units total,"[5] says Nicklos. A few months after launch, they set up production in Switzerland and Japan to try to keep up with demand. Zip Drives were flying off their shipping docks. Three years after Zip's launch, Iomega's stock soared from approximately $2.50 to $150 in real dollars. The market capitalization of the company went from $59 million before Zip in 1994 to $3.2 billion in 1997. *BusinessWeek* awarded the Zip Drive its gold medal, its highest honor for an innovative new product. And that engineer Edwards had wanted to fire? When the initial number of Iomega stock-option awards for its employees were calculated, Edwards quadrupled the amount awarded him. He made John Briggs an instant millionaire.

The intense focus of working on a blockbuster team toward a common goal is immensely rewarding for the people involved. It is an experience they usually long to re-create. It makes working meaningful and fun. "A whole bunch of other very able, very talented people are ready to do that next project," remarks Greg Allen, electrical manufacturing engineer on Zip, who is still with Iomega. "All we need to know is what 'it' is. We would do it again in a hot second."[6]

EVERYTHING, ALL AT ONCE

What did Iomega do right? The quick answer is: absolutely everything. CEO Edwards and R&D director Krieger established a clear and easily understandable vision for their new product, stuck to it, and made sure that everybody bought into the vision of the new product. The engineers did whatever it took to get from concept to reality, improvising as needed, looking to all kinds of equipment—such as the cheap rewinder—for ideas. Though they didn't all get along—engineering and marketing were practically at war in the beginning—everyone stayed focused on meeting the deadline, and so overcame interpersonal issues that might have interfered. The

CEO was a highly visible part of the team, visiting R&D regularly, and morning get-togethers over coffee with him kept everybody in the information loop. More formal meetings were true exchanges of information among different functional areas. Iomega unconsciously implemented the five practices of blockbuster success, and came up with a winner.

In the chapters to come, we will walk through each of the practices in much greater detail, but we will also show how different companies, making different kinds of products, from the personal digital assistant to toothpaste, implemented the five practices as they took their blockbusters from concept to launch.

(3) The Buck Starts Here

A Top-Down Initiative for Total Toothpaste

Harry Truman is famous for having on his desk a sign that read: "The buck stops here." We think the sign in every CEO's office should read: "The buck *starts* here."

Blockbuster products do not happen without the intense personal involvement of senior management. Usually that is the CEO— or the person who will be the next CEO or division head. Without the active participation of senior management, we found that new product development teams were unlikely to create blockbusters, a finding that challenges the advice of most management books today.

Conventional wisdom is that such day-to-day involvement amounts to *micromanagement,* and micromanagement kills the innovation process. The concept conjures up a boss who is always looking over everyone's shoulder like an annoying pest you would like to brush away, but can't. Creativity is stifled and the team's spirit is broken as well.

In contrast, *empowerment* is supposedly the correct course of action. Instead of micromanaging, the ideal senior manager should be someone who provides gentle guidance, adequate but not excessive resources, protection from outside meddlers—in other words, someone who *empowers* the team and then steps out of the way. The ideal CEO is supposed to be someone who's concerned with the big picture and whose time is spent with long-range planning and overall strategy development. The CEO lets his employees implement the strategy, make decisions, and gets involved only when problems arise.

To that we say—*baloney*. Senior management must be actively and intimately involved if the goal is blockbuster new products. This is especially true when companies embark on a new project that represents a substantial cost or a strategic redirection for the firm.[1] Yes, the job of senior management is to attend to financial dealings, human resources, and other strategic issues, but on the blockbuster teams we investigated top management *without fail* played an intimate and active role, sometimes on a day-to-day basis. Whatever title the person had within the company, from CEO to division head, he or she was in essence the project leader throughout the entire NPD process.

The involvement starts on day one. The senior manager either establishes the "must-have" features of the new product—we call them Project Pillars*—or works closely with the team as they develop them together. Then, senior managers help achieve those goals. They control the necessary resources, and give them to the team as required, and also have the authority to allow the team to break rules and cut through bureaucratic red tape.

Granted, several of our teams were small or start-up companies, and consequently having the CEO run the team was natural. But

---

* We'll take up this topic in detail in the next two chapters.

even in large companies, someone at a very senior level—a vice president or division manager, if not the CEO or chief operating officer—led the new product initiative on our blockbuster teams. See Figure 3.1.

Without question, CEO Kim Edwards was the team leader, guru, and coach that took Iomega from concept to launch with the Zip Drive. On Colgate-Palmolive's revolutionary Total toothpaste, the involvement of senior management saved the day. Which was good, because if senior management had not intensified its effort, a blockbuster product might have been shelved after its first disap-

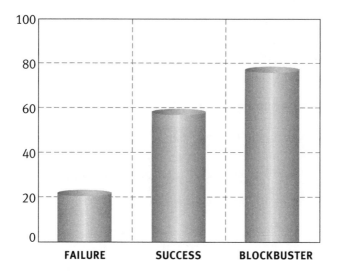

Percentage of Teams Reporting
High Levels of Management Involvement

FIGURE 3.1

Blockbusters were three and one-half times more likely to have senior management intensely involved with the new product development than the failed teams, and one-third more likely than the moderately successful ones.

pointing launch. Then senior management took an active role in the product's repositioning, and helped the team engineer a total (pun intended) turnaround. With a fresh marketing campaign and a new name, Total knocked Crest out of its three-decade position as the category leader to take over the top spot. This story is somewhat different from the other new product case histories we discuss because the action centers around marketing rather than development, demonstrating how important it is that senior management's involvement doesn't end when the new product is out the door.

A TOP-DOWN INITIATIVE FOR
COLGATE TOTAL TOOTHPASTE

In the mid-1980s, Colgate CEO Ruben Mark asked Abdul Gaffar, one of their Ph.D. chemists who holds more than a hundred patents, to develop a toothpaste that would provide long-lasting protection. Gaffar and his team of four immediately began working with the antibacterial agent triclosan, which had been around since the sixties, and was used in soaps and deodorants. The challenge was to find a way to imbed it into fresh-tasting toothpaste, and keep it from being washed away immediately. "Gum health is an evergreen goal at Colgate, so no matter what happens to budgets, you will have initiatives going towards that goal," says Kathleen Thornhill, the vice president who shepherded the launch overseas.

The breakthrough came in 1987 when Gaffar found a way to bond a polymer onto triclosan to greatly enhance its retention on teeth and gums. "It was as if we had found a way to paint in the rain—the rain being the saliva that would otherwise wash away any outside agents in the mouth," says Gaffar.

He presented his discovery at a 1988 symposium at the World

Dental Congress in Amsterdam. The good news was that since triclosan stayed active in the mouth, it could help heal gingivitis, a bleeding-gum disease that affects nearly two-thirds of the American population. Colgate officials were jubilant. "We believe this toothpaste is the biggest innovation since fluoride,"[2] said Ian Cook, president of Colgate U.S. Clinical tests abroad were even better than expected—triclosan actually worked longer than twelve hours, providing a combination of benefits that include cavity prevention, tartar control, and fresh breath.

Colgate, an American company that has been around for nearly two hundred years selling toothpaste, soap, and deodorant, is an odd duck because most of its sales have always been abroad. Consequently, it was business as usual when the company decided to market its new toothpaste overseas before it did at home. Besides, the U.S. Food and Drug Administration's go-ahead would take years of testing.

Thornhill, who had recently been promoted to vice president of global business, was in charge of rolling out Colgate's remarkable new toothpaste in six countries around the world. "Colgate takes seriously the obligation to come out with the best formulas," she says. "There was enormous enthusiasm from senior management to get it launched as quickly as we could." Although the product was designed to be revolutionary, it was not initially sold as such. The new dentifrice was launched as Colgate Gum Protection. Its vision and positioning in the marketplace changed from that of a groundbreaking product to a line extension, severely muting the message.

The launch didn't go as planned. Sales were disappointing. The market share after a few months postlaunch was only about one percent. "One percent market share for what is considered to be the best technology in toothpaste is not what you're looking for. It should have been at least five percent," says Jack Haber, then head of marketing for Spain. Was it the flavor, the advertising, or was the company not spending enough to get the word out?—all of these factors were scrutinized. "The corporate environment said that this ought to be a success, and we truly didn't know why it wasn't," says Thornhill. The market is fiercely competitive—seventy-five different varieties of toothpaste were launched during 1997 alone. In spite of this, "everybody thought it should be taking over the market," continues Thornhill.

Colgate's president, Bill Shanahan, now took a much more active role. Previously, he had only attended quarterly review meetings; postlaunch, he set up Project Gold, a worldwide team consisting of the marketing heads of several countries located around the globe to tackle rescuing the product. There were frequent conference calls and every four to six weeks the group met in New York City, flying in from Europe, Australia, South America, and Asia. Thornhill ran the meetings and immediately after would debrief Shanahan, and then she and Shanahan would meet with CEO Ruben Mark.

Market testing of the advertising concepts revealed the problem. The name "Colgate Gum Protection" emphasized "disease control," turning off many potential users, says Thornhill. Even if consumers already had bleeding gums, they didn't want to think of themselves as needing a product designed to combat periodontal disease—that was for somebody else. Furthermore, having a product with so many advantages (gingival reduction, cavity prevention, tartar control, fresh breath, and a long-lasting effect) posed a variety of problems—with so many benefits, the public didn't believe the claims.

The team had to scale back the promises of what the toothpaste could do. "People didn't believe it could work for twelve hours," says

Thornhill. "We had to find the right language to showcase the break-through of the product," she says. Senior management focused on this issue and helped solve the problem quickly. Thornhill explains:

> Having Shanahan so closely aligned—I reported directly to him, which was not typical for most new products—meant that you could make decisions quickly. All the barriers were eliminated. You could put more pressure on the ad agency. You could get more funds to do more market research in different countries quickly. If you had lots of levels between you and the top it would have been more complicated—this was a big difference in how most other projects are run. You used to have to wait to get to the end of a project, and then take senior management through the details and get them aligned with you.

Total also had to be a global brand and this added to the complexity: would what played in Paris also play in the Philippines and Peru? To find out, focus groups were held all over the world. Haber explains how it was done:

> We bundled different elements [benefits of the toothpaste] together to test, and tested them separately, and then put them together into a market simulation test. This gave us a projection of the market share—how big the product would be. We had a bundle of, say, a hundred concepts, six flavors, four colors, and we ran tests separately on each selection so that at the end of the day we had a concept, a flavor, a color, a package, a commercial.

What they learned was twofold: first, that the long-lasting protection, "the brushing that works between brushings,"[3] should be the focal point of the advertising; and second, that the name had to be changed from Gum Protection since it was too clinical sounding. Colgate Ultra and Colgate Total were the finalists. Shanahan, himself, and others at the very top "literally would sift through the research and sit through advertising development," says Thornhill. Although this level of participation by senior management was unusual at the time, she notes, it is now common at Colgate. People from the advertising agencies came to many of the meetings, another first at the time. In the end, "ultra" was thought to be an overused concept in marketing at the time, and the name was changed to Total.

"We learned that the best technology still requires superior marketing," says Thornhill. "But when we got it right, we were able to move very quickly." Colgate rolled out Total in country after country with the new name and a new ad campaign, now stressing only the twelve-hour benefit, not the protection from bleeding gums.

As the international markets were being pursued, Thornhill was made vice president of global consumer research, and Jack Haber, who had been head of marketing in Spain, was brought back to the United States as the worldwide director of consumer oral care products in 1992. His primary assignment was to make Total a worldwide success. Colgate had now committed $35 million and a team of two hundred employees to the project. Although normally someone at his level would have had oversight responsibility on such a project and kept tabs on it through a product manager, this became Haber's baby, and he rolled up his sleeves on it. He led review meetings every couple of weeks which allowed everyone on the project to get to know one another face-to-face. Additionally, he says, "every morning I called our folks in Europe and said, 'Where are we going? What's going on?' My job was to be the cheerleader, the coordinator, the problem-solver, the team builder."

Although Haber was running the show, "the president and chairman gave this project a lot of attention," he says. "They believed in this project—that's what made the difference—the energy came from the top. Their enthusiasm was transmitted through the whole company, everybody was so energized and positive."

With that kind of backing, Haber could pull out all the stops— whether that meant sending 100,000 free samples to dentists or spending millions on advertising and promotion. The team spent $20 million to promote Total to dentists alone. Haber continues, "When you want to have a new product and you know it's a hot one, should the project manager on it be somebody with two to three years of experience, or should it be someone who's been involved in this category of business for a dozen years?" The answer is obvious. You want someone with lots of experience, someone who can make decisions quickly, and who has the authority to harness the funds needed to get the job done: you need a very senior manager.

Colgate applied for FDA approval to sell the toothpaste in the United States in 1994. The next three years were devoted to two long-term studies with a thousand people. Back in Piscataway, New Jersey, Gaffar and his team were charged with creating a new flavor for the U.S. market, a mild spearmint taste that was less medicinal than the one launched worldwide. Although Gaffar was on the phone frequently with Haber, weekly meetings were held at corporate headquarters in Manhattan or in Piscataway, where the lab is located.

By the time Total had received FDA approval in 1997 to be sold as an "oral pharmaceutical"—the first toothpaste ever approved as such—it was already a star in most of the 103 countries where it was being sold. But nothing indicated the kind of reception that the dentifrice would receive here at home.

At 12:01 A.M., December 15, 1997, when Colgate opened its warehouses to begin shipping Total, trucks from the nation's largest retailers were lined up to receive their orders. Once in stores, Total jumped off the shelves: retailers reported that Total was the best-selling item in their stores—and not just among health and beauty products. It was one of the top-selling items in the entire store, sur-passing milk and bread! One month after launch, Colgate shipped 1.3 million cases, or 13 million tubes, of Total, twice what was fore-cast, and four times more than its normal product line extensions. In two months, Colgate Total had captured 10.5 percent of the U.S. toothpaste market, a remarkable feat—1 percent is equal to approxi-mately $13 million in sales.

Six months following launch, overall Colgate brand toothpaste sales were up 45 to 50 percent. For the first time since 1962, Colgate

After a disappointing initial launch under a different name, Colgate launched Total, which immediately became the number one toothpaste brand.
Photograph by Daria Amato.

wrestled the leadership position from the perennial champ, Procter and Gamble's Crest. Total has remained number one ever since in the $17 billion worldwide market.

Shortly after launch, Total received the seal of approval from the American Dental Association, as well as the Canadian and British Dental Associations. Sigmund Socransky, associate professor of oral biology at the Harvard School of Dental Medicine described Total as "one of the most remarkable oral therapeutic achievements in the past twenty years."[4]

According to Information Resources Inc., of the 767 new products it tracked in 1997, only 3 cracked the $100 million barrier—one of them was Total. Colgate as a company felt the Total impact. In 1998, Colgate's third quarter net income increased 14 percent to $214.9 million—a record for any quarter in Colgate's 195-year history.

Total was such a hit that a giant replica of a tube of it was constructed to sit alongside the company icon, a huge clock that overlooks New York's Hudson River and Manhattan from its perch in Jersey City.

With a triumph like that, many companies would normally transfer the senior manager onto the next high-priority project. But that did not happen at Colgate. More than three years after launch, Haber remains actively involved on the brand. His goal is to get "one hundred percent of the people to use Total. Then we'll go on to the next thing."

The Total project coupled a good product with active and involved senior management. Their participation—right from the very top down—proved crucial when the initial strategy with its misnamed toothpaste floundered.

WHOSE IDEA IS IT?

The kind of personal attention that Mark and Shanahan gave Total is representative of what we found on many blockbuster teams. These senior executives initiated the concept and usually formulated the main features, or Project Pillars, of the new product, as you will see in the table below. And when someone other than the CEO came up with the idea, that person typically ended up becoming a

Source of Project Pillars

APPLE IIe	Taylor Pohlman, Product Marketing Manager
HANDSPRING VISOR	Jeff Hawkins, CEO (small start-up)
IBM PC	Frank Cary, CEO
IOMEGA ZIP DRIVE	Kim Edwards, President/CEO
KODAK FUNSAVER CAMERA	Merrill Doxtader, Worldwide Distribution Manager
NOVA CRUZ XOOTR	Karl Ulrich, CEO (small start-up)
PALM PILOT 1000/5000	Jeff Hawkins, CEO (small start-up)
POLYCOM SOUNDSTATION	Brian Hinman, President/CEO (small start-up)
POWERSHOT STAPLER	Mike Marks, President, WorkTools, Inc. (small start-up company who licensed PowerShot to Black & Decker)
VECTA KART CHAIR	Bob Beck, VP of Marketing who became President

The source of several blockbusters, such as NutraSweet and some others, is not listed here because we could not determine the source of the original idea. Success (especially blockbuster success) has a thousand fathers.

top executive, either in that company or another. Examples are legion: Bob Beck was the marketing head of Vecta, a company that made computer tables, when he pushed the idea of having his company make a stackable, ergonomic chair—the phenomenal Kart chair. He later became president. David Duke at Corning wasn't the scientist who developed optic fiber in the lab, but he was the one who shepherded it to blockbuster success. He later became vice chairman of the board.

THE PRODUCT MANAGER IS KING

In contrast to most of the other blockbusters, the product marketing manager, Taylor Pohlman, and not a "senior executive" formulated the Project Pillars on the Apple IIe. Pohlman was later promoted to marketing manager of the Personal Computer Systems Division within Apple, and ultimately left to form a software company that produced such legendary products as FileMaker and PowerPoint. But at many companies, like Procter and Gamble, Microsoft, and Apple during the early 1980s, the product marketing manager or brand manager has considerable authority and autonomy and functions like a senior executive. Companies that have such a structure will find that their product managers may be their blockbuster visionaries.

WHAT DOESN'T WORK

Coming up with the idea is only the beginning. When you are the senior manager, your involvement does not stop there. Just as Colgate president Shanahan stayed the course, so did other senior managers in companies that produced blockbusters. Shanahan didn't practice "management-by-walking-around," a style in which top people in the company "pop in" unexpectedly here and there to keep tabs on what's going on and sprinkle their wisdom like stardust. Rather than being helpful, this management style when applied during new product development might better be called "hit-and-run." When the senior manager comes in to "offer" "suggestions" to a problem, and then moves on to the next crisis, the result is typically a Band-Aid solution. The suggestions are typically short-term cosmetic fixes that don't address the real underlying issues. Team members realize the problem still exists, and resent what appears to be senior management's meddling without really helping matters.

Another management style that fails for NPD is the "seldom-seen-and-rarely-heard" approach. That's when a senior executive, possibly a VP or an R&D director, provides the guiding hand at the beginning, but is conspicuously absent as the team develops the product. The team is constantly hampered by a lack of authority to move the project forward quickly—as the Total team was able to do when repositioning the dentifrice.

Lastly, a third major stumbling block to a successful NPD is senior management that constantly changes what the project is supposed to be. Sending conflicting messages to the team leads to chaos. What happened at IBM when the company tried to follow up its enormous success of the PC with a more affordable version for the home user (PC jr.) is a lesson in how this kind of constant rethinking of a project can screw it up beyond repair.

Initially the PC jr. team thought they were to develop a powerful, versatile home computer that would compete with the company's own PC at the low end of the market. It would be a computer for home use. But shortly into the project, the team learned that senior management didn't agree with that vision—they didn't want a computer that would compete with one of their own products! So they insisted that the team remove some features. Then senior management dictated that the PC jr. be completely compatible with their PC, a change that slowed development and nearly doubled the cost. Finally, there was heated internal debate at IBM about whether the company should be in the business of designing anything for the home at all, since their market niche traditionally had been *business* users and they didn't see themselves as a retail company selling to the general public. "The instant there was any problem with the program, it gave those [senior management] who felt IBM should not be in that [home] market reason to suggest that we delay the program," comments David O'Connor, who took over the project when the initial PC jr. team leader left IBM in disgust. Instead of presenting the team with a clear concept and letting them move forward, senior management provided "hit-and-run" *mis*guidance.

CLOSE ENCOUNTERS OF A BENEFICIAL KIND

While hit-and-run management fails miserably on new product development, we found that there are several useful roles that senior managers can play: project leader, technical guru, coach, and active champion. Our advice to senior management is that it doesn't matter what role you play as long as you play one of them. The choice is yours.

Project Leader

At some companies, particularly smaller ones, company presidents might spend a great deal of their day on NPD. At California-based Sequoia Voting Systems, the then president of the company, James

Hayssen, says he spent at least half his time on the development of the electronic voting machine, which debuted in 1988. "We weren't a big company—it was our lifeblood, it represented our future," he explains. The division manager, Craig Short, says, "Hayssen operated pretty much as an equal voice on the team, except when he needed to make decisions regarding financing and deadlines. He was the glue that made it happen," says Short. "He controlled the schedule from both the cost and delivery point-of-view. We were in constant communication with him, whenever we felt any issues needed resolving."

Other senior managers on blockbuster teams gave the NPD the same kind of close attention. On the Gillette Sensor razor program—which has generated some $6 billion in worldwide sales—Vice Chairman Al Zeien closely followed the team's progress and reviewed it regularly, providing his full commitment throughout, keeping team members pumped and focused.

Technical Guru

In some cases the role that senior management played on blockbusters was that of technical expert, even though it was not a role some of them envisioned for themselves when the project started. One CEO, for instance, says that he thought his role would be to go out and raise money. Instead, says Brian Hinman, the mastermind behind the Polycom SoundStation teleconferencing unit, his engineering background turned out to be immensely useful, and he ended up becoming the lead signal-processing guy for the team. Jeff Hawkins, designer of the Palm Pilot and the HandSpring Visor, was unquestionably the technical guru—as well as project leader. In fact, his title is chairman and chief product officer.

Coach

On other teams, senior managers were not technical experts driving the NPD. They were more like a coach. Here's Iomega's Kim Edwards describing what we call "management by coaching":

> The coaching aspect [of managing] is spending specific time to solve the problem. The problem may not get solved in my presence, but I get the process going, so that when I left they had a different way of looking at things. I taught them how to learn. I used to coach Little League and there are so many parallels.

Part of being a coach requires making some tough decisions, and periodically you may have to be outright autocratic. Hinman, who characterizes his role as that of a benevolent dictator, says, "You try to be collaborative, but if things seem like they are going off course, there is not a lot of time for gaining everybody's consensus."

What about *empowerment?* It is essential for blockbuster teams. Unfortunately, too often, companies do not truly empower their new product teams, frequently for good reason. Escalating vision, expanding scope, and spending more money than necessary are just some of the risks of giving a team too much authority. But there is more than one way to empower the team. In the blockbusters we studied, the teams were empowered but only because of the presence of the senior manager. The power was not given to the team; the power was on the team. To make this work, the senior manager must be someone who has the experience and authority to run the project. Jack Haber at Colgate says that he saw his job as one of "cheerleader, coordinator, problem-solver, and team builder—bringing everybody's efforts together."

Active Champion: Trust but Verify

We did find an exception to our rule of hands-on involvement. On some teams, particularly when the new product represented a technological departure such as Colgate Total, the CEO or senior manager functioned like an executive sponsor,[5] and typically provided funding to the project in "chunks." On the phenomenally successful IBM PC project, the CEO at the time, Frank Cary, got monthly reports from project director Bill Lowe and attended status review meetings. Cary would then release the next installment of cash for the project, until he became comfortable enough with the team's progress to give them the rest of the funds. We call this approach "trust but verify."

That's the kind of management support the Dustbuster team got from Black and Decker, according to marketing director on the project, Jim Martz:

> My boss's support was wonderful because he gave the project to me, and I could go to him at basically any time for anything. He was the general manager of a number of businesses, one of which this was under. There was no problem with resources whatsoever. If I needed money for research, if I needed industrial design help, I got it. . . . I could walk around and get anything done I wanted.

One caveat, however: If the trust-but-verify approach is the one your company favors, the team will more likely succeed if senior management is actively involved at the project's inception and establishes the project's parameters to control the scope of the project.

THE WELCOME MAT IS OUT

When we first saw how deeply senior management was involved in blockbuster new product development, we expected team members to say that their involvement interfered with progress. Yet when we interviewed team members, we learned that if a senior manager was willing to roll up his or her sleeves, and work right alongside everyone, that team actually welcomed the help from the top. "When you have management involved and they act quickly and give you fast decisions, that isn't interference," says Jim Martz, "that's getting crap out of the way." Corporate rules could be broken with impunity. Over at IBM, famous for its rule-bound corporate culture, Bill Lowe remembers that his team on the PC had permission to do things differently from the norm. He says:

> I spent my life growing up in staff jobs [at IBM], so I really understood the IBM process. It's very rare that you can have a Den Daddy like Frank Cary, the CEO who says, "Okay Bill, you don't have to obey the rules on this one." There was probably no one else at IBM who could tell you that.

Lastly, the senior manager's presence indicated the project's importance to the company—which kept everybody charged up and rarin' to go. People were willing to go the extra mile to get the job done. Engineer Dave Jones on the Zip Drive program, for instance, says that when any roadblocks cropped up, Krieger, the R&D director, cleared them up immediately. "I never worried about anything. . . . For two years we had a couple of guys on and off trying to figure out if we should buy a new computer

CAD/CAM system," he recalls. "And now when we said we needed one, we got bought one in the first few weeks of the program. We just picked one and we bought it." (Actually, they bought two.) With that kind of backing, you can be sure that enthusiasm for the new product remained high.

WHEN SENIOR MANAGEMENT IS MIA

What happens when a project is not registering on senior management's radar screen? That's not good. Yet that is a typical tactic—senior management is involved at the kickoff, and then pulls back and maintains a low profile until the design is complete; coming into the picture when a large financial commitment is needed to begin production, or when the product is being readied for national launch. This is how projects run into trouble.

On the IBM PC jr. project, for example, engineering manager Gary Pitt explains how the lack of support from higher up affected the team:

> It's a terrible thing to permit people—myself and the people working for me—to work so hard without more guidance. I felt myself and my team were swimming against the current, not really having the support of upper management. The only time I saw [Don] Estridge [the head of the division] was when there was a problem.

Ouch. As we said, the management style of keeping oneself distant from the day-to-day operation was not what we found on blockbuster teams. Nor did we find that "management by walking around" worked either. Instead, the active participation of a very senior manager on the project conveyed the strong and clear message that what the team was killing itself for, with long hours and late nights, was worth it. If the team succeeded, they would be praised and compensated. If they had a problem, the senior manager could help them solve it quickly.

Although this kind of day-to-day participation of senior management has been out of favor for a couple of decades, some management scholars have begun suggesting a return to this style of management.[6] In fact, one study notes that the more senior management was involved in new product development, *the more innovative the new products were.*[7] We would add: more successful, too. To use famous examples of past blockbusters, consider: Tom Watson, the former CEO of IBM, took a critical role in the development of the IBM 360, the first general-purpose mainframe computer. Akio Morita, Sony's chairman, was also the key figure in Sony's development of the Walkman. And the undying support of Charles Adams, chairman of Raytheon, for the microwave oven enabled his company to weather a twenty-plus-year development cycle to commercialize the first successful home microwave oven and transform cooking forever.

AT SOME COMPANIES, IT WAS DO OR DIE

For several of our blockbuster teams, senior management had no choice but to get deeply involved in the new product development. Their companies were in trouble, each of them relying on the new product to put the company back on solid financial footing. Think of Kim Edwards warning everyone at Iomega as they raced to develop the Zip Drive: "No Comdex, no company, no choice." The same was true at numerous other companies. At Sequoia Voting Systems, the shift from making a hand-operated voting apparatus to their electronic blockbuster literally saved the company. Craig Short comments, "Without moving forward into electronics, the company had no future—you might as well sell the thing off and make it a little mom-and-pop operation. We had substantial financial problems." A looming crisis, indeed. It pushed the company to develop a new type of electronic voting machine, one that used the press of a button to register a vote—no dimpled chads here.

But what about when it is not crisis time for a company? Does senior management still need to be involved in such a direct manner then? Yes. The lifeblood of any company is creating new and innovative products. Resting on past success and not innovating for the future is a death knell. It leads to laziness and sloppy thinking. We agree with Intel's in-house axiom: *Only the paranoid survive.* A certain atmosphere of crisis pushes people to think creatively and act decisively, and that is how blockbuster products are born.

On some of the blockbuster projects we studied, senior executives were on the team because the team was the whole company— Handspring was formed to make a better Palm Pilot; Polycom, today the absolute leader in teleconferencing equipment worldwide, was formed to develop a better unit than anything available at the time; a tiny little company called Nova Cruz came into existence to make the runaway success that is the Xootr scooter. But whether the product is the company's only focus or not—and Colgate-Palmolive is without question the opposite of Nova Cruz—senior management's participation every step of the way was instrumental to the ultimate success of the new products.

Effective senior management starts right at the beginning of any NPD, creating the vision of the project and giving the team the necessary resources to do the job. By being an active participant in the process, the senior manager allows the team to cut through layers of bureaucracy to make decisions quickly to reach the desired goal: a new product that beats the competition and amazes the consumer. But before this can happen, a good idea has to go from vague concept to definite, firm parameters, those Project Pillars we've mentioned. How to do that is the next subject we take up.

(4) Clear and Stable Vision (Part 1)

Building Project Pillars at Polycom

Having a great idea of the product-to-be is naturally a key element in creating a blockbuster. But a great idea alone is not enough to ensure success. Your chances of turning a good idea into a whopping success go up dramatically if you thoughtfully formulate specific parameters of what the product will be. We call these parameters *Project Pillars.* Think of them as the "must-haves" of your new product, the immutable principles that provide guidance and direction for the team. They differ from specifications that focus on product features, because Pillars encompass benefits as well as constraints—and what the product will *not* be.[1]

Project Pillars must be easily understandable, agreed to by both senior management and the team, and remain stable until you offer the product for sale. Changing them midstream dispirits the team, leads to conflict among team members, will probably hold up production, and will most likely result in the new product crashing in the marketplace. Thus, the second practice of blockbuster product development is: articulate clear Project Pillars that remain stable.

We found that most of the blockbusters in our database scored high in establishing a clear vision with stable Project Pillars throughout development. Blockbuster teams were more than three times more likely to excel in having a clear and stable vision than the failed teams, and 1.4 times more likely than the moderately successful ones. (See Figure 4.1.)

CLEAR AND STABLE VISION AT POLYCOM

The story of how a start-up company, Polycom, created the first truly useable conference phone, the SoundStation, demonstrates how crucial stable Project Pillars are to a team's success:

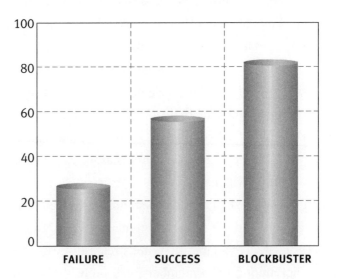

Percentage of Teams with a Clear and Stable Vision

FIGURE 4.1

Blockbuster vision requires the creation of product parameters, or Project Pillars, that must be in place at the outset of a project. Most important was that the teams did not waver from this vision once it was established.

Imagine it is 1985 and you and a group at the home office need to have a conference call with someone at a division in another location. Your group is gathered around a clunky-looking device sitting on a conference room table; so is the guy in another city. When the meeting begins, people speak into the apparatus on the table, but the responses of the distant participant come from speakers around the perimeter of the room. The sound is tinny. Often the voice from the speakers turns into a screech that obscures what was just said. When two people speak at once, one of them is cut off, and those at the other end of the line are understandably confused—*what did he just say?* Yet the equipment you're using was advertised as having full-duplex sound, meaning that more than one person's voice could be heard at a time without one being "clipped" out. Ha! you're thinking, full-duplex audio is more fiction than fact. In short, teleconferencing was a mess.

By the early 1990s, if your company believed in the value and could afford the cost, it invested in what seemed like a great idea: a videophone that allowed you to see as well as hear the people at another location. The gee-whiz aspect of actually seeing the person you were talking to so impressed users that nobody paid much attention to the poor audio quality, but it was still awful. Yet few CEOs (who had shelled out between $60,000 to $100,000, plus extra for camera, lights, cables) wanted to focus on what didn't work.

Brian Hinman was one of those who knew that teleconferencing equipment was largely ineffective—even though his own company made videophones. When he was a twenty-two-year-old engineering whiz, he co-founded PictureTel. Now his company was spending its resources trying to perfect the video, but, he notes, "the complaints were actually about the audio."

He knew because he used teleconferencing equipment himself

that was a step above the others, the NEC VoicePoint, but it still left much to be desired. Here's how he describes his experience with it:

> At the time we were doing a joint development with Intel in Princeton. The guy who was doing the chip effort was splitting his time between the Boston area [where PictureTel was located] and Princeton. When he was in Princeton, there was no videoconferencing, but he had a phone. To tie him into project meetings, I put the NEC VoicePoint in the middle of my conference room in the engineering department, and I went to his office and got a photo of this guy, and put his picture in the middle of the table. We could all look at him sitting next to the speakerphone, and we'd all hear him on the speakerphone. So, I thought, I'm getting most of the value here of a videoconference with just having a decent quality full-duplex speakerphone.

The NEC product, however, was far from perfect. Though sold as full-duplex equipment, it really didn't hit the mark. "If you moved it, the audio would start feeding back and howling, and the power cord would fall out and disconnect," he remembers, "but I thought, there's a pony in there." He knew that video was not the key, *but rather it was the ability of the group to carry on a normal conversation with the absent participant.*

Hinman was his own first customer. He knew that what people like himself wanted in teleconferencing was full-duplex audio, and he realized that video was expensive and unnecessary. Always the entrepreneur, Hinman left PictureTel in the late summer of 1990 to start a new company—one that would make better teleconferencing equipment. He moved to the West Coast, and brought in an alum of PictureTel who earlier had moved back to his native California, Jeff Rodman. With money from venture capitalists, they set up shop in Menlo Park in the spring of 1991. Their goal was to build a better mousetrap—that mousetrap being a first-rate teleconferencing system.

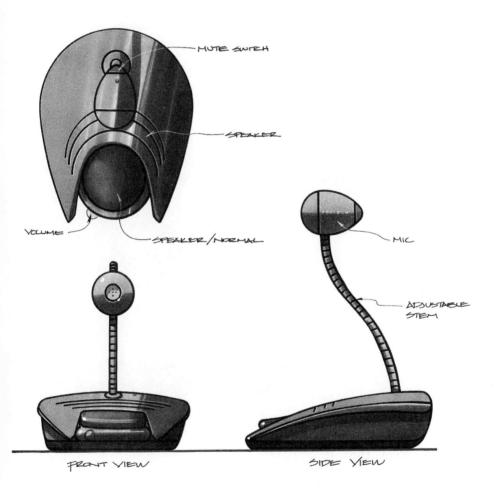

This was one of the early concepts for the Polycom teleconferencing phone. It used a microphone seemingly suspended in space on an adjustable stem. This concept was rejected because there was concern regarding the stem's durability and the feeling that the design was too far out. Illustration courtesy of Polycom.

Polycom, as they named their new company, had a shaky start. The first product in development was a desktop speakerphone that promised improved audio. Approximately five by seven inches across and three inches high, Gumby, as employees nicknamed it, only lacked eyes and arms to resemble the cartoon character. But Gumby could only be used on a single telephone line with a headset, so it was not a true teleconferencing unit, and the technology was proving pricey. "It would have to retail for about $400, and a single-user $400 speakerphone wasn't going to find a lot of takers," says Rodman.

This was Gumby, Polycom's first prototype that customers rejected.
Photograph by Daria Amato.

When Hinman and Rodman talked to prospective customers and told them what they were going to charge for Gumby, they'd say, " 'You've got to be crazy; I can get a speakerphone for $69,' " Rodman recalls. Team members, in addition to customers, had their doubts. He continues, "People would stop me in the hall, and say,

'Who's going to buy this at that price?' You found yourself selling your own product to your employees a couple times a week."

Within a couple of months it was clear to everyone that Gumby was a loser. By late summer Hinman knew Polycom had to go head-to-head with the NEC product, but they would do it better—much better—and cheaper. In the early 1990s, the NEC VoicePoint sold for $2,500. Some cursory market research led Hinman and Rodman to believe—mistakenly it would turn out—that NEC was selling 25,000 units a year. That seemed like a lot, but they didn't question the numbers. They figured that they could build a multiuser conference phone with full-duplex sound for about half the cost of the VoicePoint, and still make a decent profit.

Hinman, along with a couple of other Polycom executives, took their vision of the new product (better than the competition, and cheaper) and formulated three must-haves—which became their Project Pillars. They were:

1. It would have superb audio quality, that is, true full-duplex capability, allowing more than one person at a time to speak and still be understood.

2. It would be easy to use. No confusing arrays of buttons and cords.

3. It would be "first-class," that is, it would look like a device that *belonged* in an executive conference room.

At this point, Hinman was quickly leaving the "fuzzy front-end" of product development, a phase that includes everything from conception to budget approval for the project.[2] The ultimately successful story of the Polycom SoundStation continues in the next chapter, after we've established what constitutes "sound" Project Pillars.

This was Polycom's original SoundStation, which
became a hit in the marketplace. In contrast to Gumby, the
SoundStation was designed for groups rather than individuals.
Photograph by Daria Amato.

TO SEE THE END, YOU MUST
HAVE A CLEAR BEGINNING

The Pillars on the Polycom SoundStation possessed two qualities
that we found over and over on other blockbuster products: clarity
and stability. When we began our research, we had no idea that they
would be so absolutely critical. Of all the five practices that go into
making blockbusters, having clear and stable Project Pillars is the
most important of all practices. Two exceptions to this rule are radically new products whose final form and application cannot be
known at the beginning, a topic we take up in Chapter 9; and products that are the result of a fortuitous accidental discovery, such as
NutraSweet, Teflon, and penicillin. With the latter, the Pillars can

emerge almost immediately upon the *eureka!* moment or take months or years to surface.

What constitutes effective Project Pillars? As we have stated, they are the must-haves of the NPD. They include the basic benefits to the customer, and also incorporate constraints that originate from the engineering, manufacturing, finance, marketing, and legal departments.

In Chapter 2, you saw how Iomega's Kim Edwards articulated five Project Pillars of the Zip Drive: it had to (1) store 100 megabytes, (2) be just "fast enough," (3) list for no more than $300 for an external drive, and less for an internal drive, (4) be ridiculously simple to install, and (5) be ready in time to show at Comdex. The table below shows how several other blockbuster teams defined their Project Pillars.

You can see that Project Pillars must be specific enough to give guidance to the team, but allow for some flexibility to keep team members interested and their creativity stimulated. The SoundStation went through several permutations before the team settled on the final star-shaped form. And look at the two Pillars the IBM team had: beat Apple (with a PC) and do it in one year. Plenty of room there for creativity. Pillars are a foundation, but what is built on them—the product's specifications—can change during development.

Blockbuster Project Pillars

PRODUCT	PILLARS	SCOPE
AASTRA WAVESTAR DIGITAL VIDEO SYSTEMS (FORMERLY LUCENT)	▶ Same functions as the previous generation of products ▶ Substantial space and cost reduction ▶ Demo the product at their annual trade show ▶ Deliver product to customers by May 1	Performance, manufacturing, features

PRODUCT	PILLARS	SCOPE
APPLE IIe	▶ Simplify manufacturing ▶ Modernize ▶ Reduce cost ▶ Look like the Apple II	Manufacturing, performance, cost, form
CORNING OPTIC FIBERS	▶ Lowest cost per bit	Cost
GE CAT SCANNER	▶ Develop a breakthrough that would leapfrog EMI	Competition, performance
HANDSPRING VISOR	▶ $149 for base model ▶ Use Palm Operating System and USB connection	Price, benefit, compatibility
IBM PC	▶ Beat Apple ▶ Do it in one year	Competition, performance, time
IOMEGA ZIP DRIVE	▶ Store 100 megabytes ▶ "Fast enough" ▶ Sell for $200–$300 for an external drive, less for an internal drive ▶ Ridiculously simple to install ▶ Ready for Comdex	Performance, price, form, time
KODAK FUNSAVER CAMERA	▶ Use 35mm film ▶ Packaged in a cardboard box ▶ Cost under $2 ▶ Use a specific developing process ▶ Cut development time to 7 months ▶ Better than Ektralite*	Compatibility, form, manufacturing, price

* The Ektralite camera was Kodak's high volume 110 camera. The company sold hundreds of thousands of them at the time.

PRODUCT	PILLARS	SCOPE
MARVIN DOUBLE-HUNG WINDOWS	▶ Beautiful ▶ Good performance ▶ Look like wood	Appearance, performance
MOTOROLA STARTAC PHONE	▶ Must be "wearable"	Form
NOVA CRUZ XOOTR SCOOTER	▶ Transparent to public transportation ▶ Easily carried into stores or work ▶ Faster than walking ▶ Cool, not geeky	Appearance, features, performance
PALM PILOT	▶ Fits in pocket ▶ Synchronizes seamlessly with PC ▶ Fast and easy to use ▶ No more than $299	Form, performance, function, price
POLYCOM SOUNDSTATION	▶ Full-duplex sound quality good or better than competition ▶ Simple to use ▶ Looks "first-class"	Performance, competition, form, appearance
POWERSHOT STAPLER	▶ Simple to use ▶ Visually distinctive	Performance, appearance
VECTA KART CHAIRS	▶ High reliability ▶ Long life cycle ▶ Cheap to manufacture	Customer benefits, time, performance, manufacturing

FINDING YOUR PROJECT PILLARS

So how can you come up with the Pillars for a great new project? We will talk about this a great deal more in the next chapter, but we need to take a look at first things first. How teams—and visionaries— actually formulated the vision of their new product initially puzzled us, but when we reevaluated our interview notes, and conducted additional follow-up interviews, a pattern emerged. We found that the visionaries (a) perceived a need for a new product, and then (b) collected information from both customers and competitors. To help you develop the Pillars for your next project, we've put together a "dirty dozen" list of questions to ask yourself:[3]

1. What is the product's "reason for being"?

2. At what level of excellence must that main benefit be delivered?

3. What features must be present?

4. What are the design constraints from engineering, manufacturing, marketing?

5. In what critical comparison points must this product excel vis-à-vis the competition?

6. How will it differ from the competition?

7. How is it better than the competition?

8. Is this difference/improvement meaningful to the target market?

9. Who is the specific target market for this product?

10. Can you characterize the ideal customer for your product (age, income, lifestyles for a consumer product; size, geography, level of service for an industrial product)?

11. How big is the potential market for your product?

12. Are there schedule constraints, such as a trade show, Christmas season?

Answering these questions requires that you analyze and try out competitive products, and really understand who your customer is and what he or she needs—in short, you must become an expert on the market as well as the technology. This period of ferment[4] cannot be skipped over. It takes study, observation, analysis, time, patience, foresight, and . . . a great idea. Think of those months when the Polycom team mucked around with Gumby. That's the kind of "fermenting" we're talking about. After you feel assured that you've done all the required research and rumination, the Pillars for your project should naturally emerge.

Hold That Line: Stability Rules

Once you have formulated your Pillars, you have to hold the line against the temptation to change them before the product is offered for sale. That may sound easy, but doubt and second-guessing occurs all too often, and is the downfall of many a failed project. To avoid what's called "vision creep," everyone on the team needs to completely buy into the concept. All must agree that fulfilling the Pillars is the goal, just as a sports team needs to agree that scoring is the goal. An undercurrent of constant questioning about the validity of the Pillars will destroy the project well before it gets off the ground.

Two projects at IBM—one successful, one a failure—illustrate the impact of vision buy-in and stability. On the enormously successful IBM PC the original Pillars of the project (beat Apple and do it in one year) were so stable that 80 percent of the charts used in the first presentation to obtain approval for the project were used again at the final meeting to get the go-ahead for launch. Engineering director Bill Syndnes recalls, "We never allowed the schedule to change. Never. Did we make every milestone on it? No way. Did we make the end point? You betcha." Halfway through the project the initial team director, Bill Lowe, was promoted to run a division. The individual who succeeded him, Don Estridge, talked to Lowe frequently about the project. Lowe vividly remembers what Estridge said to him after the final presentation: "He said, 'I told them that if we hadn't stuck with these initial assumptions and not changed them, there's no way that we could have gotten it done in a year."

The IBM PC was an immediate hit. Introduced in 1981 at retail outlets, IBM sold 35,000 by the end of the year, five times the estimate. It would become a legend in the industry and would effectively knock Apple out of its front-runner position. Beat Apple? It did.

But remember what happened on the IBM PC jr. when senior management kept changing course? The project began almost as soon as the PC was launched, but this time, the team never had firm Pillars that everyone—team members as well as senior management—agreed to. The result was constant bickering over what the product really *was* as well as who it was *for*. Without ever resolving these issues, the vision of the PC jr. changed several times before launch. Initially, it was to be a computer primarily for games and not compatible with its big sister, the PC. Then senior management decided to take away some functions so that it would not cannibalize the low end of the PC market. As the vision changed, they tried to gear it to *both* the home as well as business market. The Project Pillars? They were like leaves blowing in the wind. The PC jr. tanked as soon as it was introduced.

WHAT PROJECT PILLARS ARE NOT

While Project Pillars of course should meet customer needs, Pillars are not—repeat *not*—a response to every customer's whim and desire, which can change like the flavor of the month. Yes, you need to get customer feedback, and you should get it from a variety of customers. But one customer may ask for a specific feature that doesn't coincide with what others want or need. We heard many complaints in our interviews from engineers and designers about how marketing personnel would push and pull them during development. Marketers would go to a customer who would say he loved the new product concept, but needed it in orange instead of basic black. The marketers would come back and insist that the designers reconfigure the product in orange, and senior management would agree. Then in a month or so, the marketers would come back and say that another customer was insisting that he would buy the product if only it were in blue, and once again the marketers would insist that it be made in blue. Arghh!

Once the Project Pillars are set, you have to resist (or at least filter) some pretty strong "suggestions," as did former R&D director at Johnson and Johnson, Steve Savitz. During the development of a new bench-top coagulation unit, the Koagulab-16S, which analyzes how quickly blood clots, both marketers and sales reps kept coming up with bright ideas to "improve" it. "Sometimes a marketing or senior management guy says, 'If you add this, it would be great,' " Savitz observes. "Or the sales director says, 'If you did that, it would sell twice as fast.' But I never let these get too far. I cut them off before it got to the team." Savitz says he had learned his lesson on earlier projects where the specifications kept changing, and the products were bombs. "All we did was slow down the launch of those products," he asserts. "Getting a new product to market is critical. You can always make changes later."

By holding the line on the Pillars, Savitz nursed a blockbuster to market. When it debuted in 1986, the Koagulab-16S enabled J&J to offer a systems solution to blood analysis, selling both the equipment to run the test and the necessary chemical reagent. It increased J&J's hardware and reagents sales by close to 20 percent. Had Savitz given in to the many suggestions he was hearing from the marketing and sales force, it's unlikely the product would have been such a success.

Changing the Pillars would undoubtedly have delayed the introduction of the Koagulab, but there's another danger lurking in the bushes of customer commentary: it can sometimes point you in the wrong direction. Although you are designing products that your customers supposedly want, you may hear suggestions that are impossible to implement for any number of reasons—cost, technical limitations, manufacturing difficulties, legal constraints. In trying to satisfy these blue-sky suggestions, the team ends up going off on a tangent that leads nowhere, but uses up time and valuable company resources. Yet when you hear customers' wish lists, you may be so anxious to please that it's difficult to sort out what to listen to, and what to ignore. Innovation scholar Eric von Hipple recommends that when talking with lead users[5] you try to limit their suggestions to avoid ideas that are outside the realm of possibility. Yes, we would all like a Star Trek transporter in our basement, but is that realistic? Can working on a wild suggestion help guide the new product effort? Or will it take you down a dead end street? Resisting changes to the Project Pillars is not the same as listening to a lead customer inform you and your team about design specs that fall within the range of the Pillars, a topic we'll explore in detail in the next chapter.

WHAT'S SO HOT ABOUT PROJECT PILLARS, ANYWAY?

You may be asking yourself, "What is so new about Project Pillars?" The concept of having a firm vision and sticking to it is obvious, a bit like motherhood and apple pie. But teams often get sidetracked, and change the vision, because the Project Pillars have not been clearly articulated, formalized, or agreed to by everyone on the team. We recommend: create the Pillars and change them at your peril.

If your project is *not* proceeding as you would like, conduct the following simple exercise. If your team is on the right track, it will take only fifteen minutes. During one of your team meetings, ask the group to describe the project vision and the Pillars, but not verbally. Have everyone write them out on a sheet of paper anonymously. Give them five minutes and no more. If someone asks for more time, you probably have a problem. Then, collect the responses and as a group take ten minutes to compare them. If the responses match, you and your team are in synch. If not, spend a half hour or so seeking agreement. If you cannot reach consensus, either have a division manager, or someone higher, clearly formulate the Pillars, or ask the team to get additional information. Have key people on the team visit several customers preferably together; reanalyze competitive products, their strengths and limitations; or use the products themselves if appropriate. Then, and only then, formulate new Project Pillars, and make sure they are clear, understandable, and that everyone agrees to them.

Once the Project Pillars are established, post them; possibly have them printed on memo pads for the team. Don't ignore them or lose sight of them. As Yogi Berra says, "If you don't know where you're going, you might wind up somewhere else."

Winding up "somewhere else" is not how products become blockbusters.

(5) Clear and Stable Vision (Part 2)

Building Your Own Project Pillars

By now you must be asking, how can I come up with Project Pillars for a blockbuster product? Do I just stare off into space and see what bright ideas I get?

Of course not. We found that the visionaries and teams who created blockbusters followed a distinct, identifiable process that started with knowing the customer's needs inside and out. Sometimes it was because the visionary with the concept was the customer himself, like Brian Hinman of Polycom. But as we continue the story of the SoundStation, we see that he didn't rely only on his opinion of what the teleconferencing equipment should be. He went to important customers to hear what they had to say about it. He made sure he and his team had what we call *consummate customer empathy,* that is, knowing exactly what your customers need and want—and will eagerly buy.

THE SOUNDSTATION, CONTINUED

Hinman wasn't ready to commit all the company's resources to the new product without a good deal of customer input—a mistake he says he made at PictureTel. So he sent Ed Burfine, Polycom's marketing and sales VP, all over the country that fall with the Gumbylike prototype to show prospective customers and learn exactly what features they would want in a better speaker-phone. "I called on ten major users of teleconferencing in the U.S., a broad cross-section from major corporations like Goldman Sachs and the Ford Motor Company to state governments and universities, people we thought would span our market space," Burfine says.

What did he find?

Not only did our new product have to work flawlessly in full-duplex mode; it had to be on target with the human factors and associated functions. We learned for instance that the government and legal communities wanted to be able to record directly. It [the new unit] had to interact with PBX and key telephone systems. It had to have a minimal keypad. It also had to not overreact if you put a coffee cup down next to it, or if someone in the room crinkled a piece of paper.

Burfine came back with good information that others hadn't thought about—who knew that the ability to record the conversation would be important to some customers? But not until one particular potential customer was in the picture would the final design gel. Understand, the customer was a big one—Intel, one of the top makers of computer processors in the world. With offices all over the globe, Intel was one of the largest users of audio-conferencing equipment in the country. Hinman, who conducted the interview with this important customer describes what happened:

> The guy who was managing the conferencing infrastructure at Intel happened to have been a product-marketing guy. He was listening to us talk about our new teleconferencing equipment, and he says, "Let me tell you what we don't like about the speakerphone we're using now. We don't like the speaker on the side of the room because everybody keeps turning their heads and screaming to it, which is nonsensical, but that's what they do. We don't like having to set the call up on the side of the room and then transfer it over and sit down. We're busy people. We book these rooms back to back, and we want to come in, sit down, dial a call, and leave. . . . Let me tell you what we want." He then spent a half hour mapping out a product for us—the physical configuration of how the product should sit on the table, why it should have a keypad right on the unit, how the speaker and microphone had to be in the center, how it went on and off line, where the lights should be. He walked us through, step by step. . . . And we thought about what he said long and hard, because his concept was different than what we were doing. But we decided to build what Intel was asking for—button for button and light for light.

Hinman says that after that meeting, they actually cut back on some features in order to make the unit so simple that no one would ever say they didn't know how to use it. "We knew that people do not get trained on conferencing equipment," he adds. "We realized we would have to dumb it down to the point where it would actually have fewer features than your desktop telephone. If you look at the original model, it doesn't have a lot of buttons. That wasn't because we didn't know what buttons to put on it—we intentionally took buttons off to make it deadly simple."

Because it needed a different form and function, it couldn't look anything like the unfortunate Gumby. So Polycom splurged on spe-

One of Polycom's sixteen concept sketches demonstrating the product's new form and better function for larger groups. The drawback of this concept was that it looked big on a conference room table. Illustration courtesy of Polycom.

cial paint to give people the feeling that it must be made of titanium or another equally expensive material instead of plastic. The Sound-Station would be a first-class piece of equipment that would sit in the middle of your conference table, speakers and microphones in a single unit shaped like a futuristic, three-pointed star. Not only would it be the answer to the problems experienced in the past; it would be a status symbol as well.

Polycom selected this concept for further development. One of its advantages was the seemingly smaller footprint. Another was an overall feeling that it just looked better. Illustration courtesy of Polycom.

The venture capitalists, a notoriously unforgiving group, were keen on the new product direction, and so were the engineers, who immediately bought into the new vision—in contrast to how they felt about Gumby. In spite of the enthusiasm for the new product, Hinman wanted to confirm it with other potential users. So that winter, he and Burfine visited the conference managers of several Fortune 500 companies—*would they be interested in this exciting new teleconferencing equipment?*

They got what they were after, that elusive *hot yes!** that means *Yes! I want to buy it!* Once Hinman and Burfine had a prototype of the new unit to show, many said that they would buy it right then and there. Intel placed an order for 600 units. "The question you have to ask is, 'If we do what you're suggesting, are you going to buy this?'" Hinman reflects. "And if the answer is, 'Well, no, I'm just talking,' that's very different than saying, 'Yes, I'll buy this.'"

The reception the SoundStation received would have warmed the heart of any venture capitalist or entrepreneur, but now Hinman and his team needed to know how big the market was. Was it an elephant or a mouse? Instead of ordering up an elaborate marketing report—their company didn't have the capital anyway—they relied on a simple but time-tested analysis, the kind you do at lunch on the back of a napkin. From some published data, Hinman and his two top honchos, Rodman and Burfine, figured that there were approximately two million conference rooms in the United States. And remember, they had heard that the competition was selling around 25,000 units a year at $2,500 a pop.

---

* A *hot yes!* is a phrase coined by one of our blockbuster team leaders. You'll read more about it in the next chapter.

"We felt as confident as one can in these circumstances, given that we projected a product at half the price, with better performance, much easier to use, more forgiving of conference-room problems, and better looking," Rodman says. "Either we would grow to a comparable share with 25,000 units a year at a list price of $1,195— yielding $15 million in revenue—or we might SWAG a conservative one percent of those two million conference rooms, showing 20,000 units per year—yielding $12 million in revenue." Either way, this one felt like a winner.

It needed to. Venture capital would soon run out. "Getting a loan from venture capitalists is not like getting a loan from Mom," reminds Rodman. Unlike Mom, who will continue believing in you until the last dollar is gone, venture capitalists can pull the plug anytime, and often do—if they think their money is going down the proverbial sinkhole. The SoundStation was the company's hope for salvation, but numerous technical problems lay ahead, not the least of which was that the software for effective full-duplex sound did not yet exist. Yet that was why the group of fifteen or so engineers, bright kids just out of school as well as seasoned veterans, had joined Polycom to work long hours and create something innovative—and make a killing with stock options if the company went public. Plus, they had no choice; they would either make this new product work, or close up shop and go home. Were they committed to the Project Pillars? You can be sure they were.

The deadline to ship Intel's order that summer was approaching and the pressure on the team was intense. As Hinman recalls:

This was a painful time. Although the mechanicals and hardware were done, we were spinning out new code for software just about every other day, and we were working night and day on it. We

were confronted with what were at times seemingly insurmountable technical problems. You'd go home and think about it, and
come back in the morning and say, *Let's try this.* You'd just keep
flogging at it month after month after month. And as the summer
was ticking by, we were starting to lose credibility with the customer [Intel], and that caused more pressure to get the thing fin-
ished. But the deadline helped focus and motivate the team to hit
the ship date.

There was another deadline on the horizon. Telecon, the annual
trade show in Anaheim was in mid-August, and they damn well
needed to be there with their product. Burfine remembers being at
Polycom's booth the day before Telecon opened, not quite in
despair, but none too happy, either. The posters were up, the
brochures printed, the SoundStation model looked good, but . . . the
digital code for the full-duplex audio quality still wasn't working
right. What they did have was marginal at best. "Then I heard we got
it," he says, "and Jeff flew down with the chip, popped it in the case,
and Boom! It worked."

A month later, Polycom shipped its SoundStations to Intel. It
was a remarkable feat for a start-up that had spent the first five
months working on a product that had to be dumped. Total elapsed
time from development to launch: one year. In all, Intel bought
1,500 in the first year. That original estimate of how many NEC
VoicePoints were sold? "After we started shipping we found out that
the sales of the competitive speakerphones were actually only about
3,000 units a year," Rodman says, not 25,000. "If we had known that
earlier, we would probably never have proceeded with the
SoundStation—this is a good illustration of the motivational power
of misinformation," he adds wryly.

Now that they had a true full-duplex teleconferencing unit, the SoundStation had to overcome the bad press of other teleconferencing equipment that failed to deliver on a full-duplex claim. Burfine remembers convincing Harry Newton, the influential editor of the old *Teleconnect* magazine, that the SoundStation was vastly superior to the competition. "He didn't believe me," says Burfine, "so I told him to go to another room to make the call, and I'd talk to him from under the table. I go under the table, the SoundStation is on top, and I'm talking and he can hear me. I buried my head in the corner—that's always a problem—and it performed the way we said it would. He became a convert and gave us a full-page rave review." Burfine would repeat his show-and-tell many times, demonstrating to potential customers in Hong Kong and Sydney and London and New York and Detroit how well the SoundStation worked—that

The deluxe Polycom SoundStation Premier, coupled with the original SoundStation introduced two years before, cemented the company's leadership position in the audio conferencing market for a decade.
Photograph by Daria Amato.

people in a teleconference could speak freely back and forth without distortion, echoes, or having entire words and entire phrases blocked out by another voice.

The following spring, Burfine signed up an important client, British Telecom. Polycom would build SoundStations and put the British Telecom label and logo on it. No detail was too small for Hinman's exacting attention, down to the British Telecom logo. Numerous thumbnail-sized logos were rejected before Hinman finally approved one. "To have a blockbuster product, you have to do everything right," Burfine adds. "It has to be world-class in performance, in human factors, in design, pricing, distribution. Every single detail is important."

The team's diligence paid off. From September 1992 to the end of the year, Polycom sold more than 3,000 units—exceeding the combined yearly sales of all other teleconference phones. Since then, more than one million SoundStations have made their way to conference rooms all over the world. Winner of numerous design and technical awards, the SoundStation was one of *BusinessWeek*'s best new products of the 1990s, winning the Design of the Decade award. By all measures, the SoundStation is a blockbuster.

The SoundStation not only saved Polycom; it propelled the company to stardom status. Polycom has since grown into the world's largest provider of video and audio conferencing equipment. Along the way, Polycom acquired several other companies, including Hinman's old company, PictureTel, in 2001.

Throughout the entire process, Hinman and his team stayed true to the original vision and Project Pillars. And when it came down to determining precisely what features the equipment should have, they listened to the customer.

CONSUMMATE CUSTOMER EMPATHY

We found that the basic idea for a product almost always occurs because the visionary has intimate knowledge of the customer. Sometimes he is the customer himself. Sometimes he conducts in-depth interviews at the customers' location—and he may even stay there for a day or more. We'll take a look at each of these ways of gaining consummate customer empathy.

You Are the Customer

We found that the *eureka!* moment often occurred when the individual actually lived in the environment where the innovative new product would be used. In effect, they were their own first customers.

Hinman, for example, wanted better teleconferencing equipment, so he built it. Edwards wouldn't bother putting the old Iomega Bernoulli Box together because it was too complicated, and he wanted a product that was simpler to use. It's the same with so many of the other blockbuster products; in fact, it's so often the case that we've come to think of this as the Golden Rule of Blockbuster New Product Development: *You are your own first best customer.* You would buy and use your product if it were available.

Guy Kawasaki, one of the first Apple employees and a highly regarded Silicon Valley venture capitalist, says unequivocally, "If you want to create a revolutionary new product, design something that you yourself would use." He explains why:

> A lot of people design products from a standpoint of, well, Dataquest predicts that the market for Internet software will be

twenty billion in two years, or the demographics for our market are thirty-five-year-olds, 2.1 children, drives a Volvo, has a $50,000 annual income. A lot of new product development is done with the mind-set of, "There is a market out there and the research proves it." That's bullshit. Yet you could make the case, that if you design the product for yourself, how do you know there are more people like you out there? But at least you know there is *one* person for sure who would use this, and that is one more than any market research could guarantee.

Amen. Steve Wozniak, the computer genius behind Apple, designed the legendary Apple I for himself. "I knew that this box wasn't what other people called a computer, but it was what I needed anyway," he remembers. "I did it exactly the way I wanted."

We heard this repeatedly in our interviews: designers of blockbuster products were making products *they* wanted. The well-known story of Post-it notes is a case in point. Art Frye, coinventor of Post-its, used little slips of paper to keep track of places in his hymnal when he sang in the church choir, but they would sometimes fall out just as he needed the page. Solution? A little strip of not-so-sticky adhesive on the note paper.

You bet Art Frye was among the first users of Post-its, just as was the inventor of that hot little scooter for young-at-heart urban dwellers, Karl Ulrich. Ulrich was a business professor when he came up with his bright idea in January of 1999. "I spent most of my adult life on college campuses," he says. "At MIT, I had one office in the artificial intelligence lab and one in the Sloan School, and was always making that trip, about three-quarters of a mile." He wanted a vehicle that would get him from building to building quickly. A bike was speedy, all right, but you had to lock it up and unlock it at both ends, a bothersome chore he wanted to eliminate. He wanted something smaller that could be picked up and carried inside the building. He wanted something that could easily be carried on public transportation. He wanted something environmentally friendly.

One day he read an article on Pixar Animation, the group that made the movie *Toy Story*. In the accompanying photo, a Pixar employee was riding around on a scooter. Although it was a kid's scooter, not big enough for an adult, the light bulb in Karl's mind went off, and he instantly knew what his adult scooter should look like. That day he emailed his brother Nathan, who has a mechanical engineering firm in New Hampshire, outlining the basic idea of a two-wheeled kick scooter for adults in four Project Pillars. The new scooter should be:

1. Transparent to public transportation—able to carry it on buses, trains, etc.

2. Easily carried into a store or an office.

3. Faster than walking.

4. Cool looking and not geeky.

And that is exactly what the Xootr became. The vision and Project Pillars never wavered from what Karl Ulrich put down in that first email to his brother. Sold through the Internet by midsummer of 1999—only six months later—the Xootr took off in 2000 when *Time* magazine dubbed it the "Rolls-Royce of scooters." While the privately held company keeps exact sales figures secret, a spokesperson says they have sold "tens of thousands," through their Dover, New Hampshire, factory, and have distribution arrangements in several countries. To be fair, the Xootr's success also owes something to good timing, as it came out just as children's scooters were taking off.

The chronicles of successful products are time after time stories of designers designing for themselves. Let's go back to Apple, whose early products were huge hits in the market. Apple was the first computer company that used its own technology to run the company, and thus all employees were completely familiar with their computers. They knew what kind of tasks and data their computer could handle well, and what it couldn't. They could see a problem before they received sales reports. Although Apple II went to market with only an upper case-typeface, THE NEED FOR A LOWER-CASE FONT QUICKLY BECAME APPARENT TO APPLE EMPLOYEES AS WRITING IN ALL UPPER-CASE SENDS A HYPERCHARGED MESSAGE. The glitch was soon fixed so that people could have calmer copy.

But Apple's batting average, as most students of high tech know, isn't perfect. They didn't follow their own admonition to design for themselves. When they launched a computer called Lisa, they themselves were using a souped-up model with lots more RAM than what they offered to the public. Customers complained that they couldn't run large programs. Lisa engineers were puzzled—they had plenty of space on *their* hard drives. Their own machines had twice as much RAM and two to four times the hard-drive capacity than you could buy in a Lisa retail. Moral? *Only sell to others what you would buy yourself.*

Go, Look, and Listen

Sometimes, however, you can't be the customer. Or even if you are the customer, you must appeal to many different kinds of customers, not just yourself, if you are to have a blockbuster. You must find a way to really get in synch with your target buyers, to find out what they want in a new product—or what they could want—when they themselves may not know, or be able to verbalize it.

Developing this kind of consummate customer empathy is never going to happen in a telephone conversation with a customer, no matter how chatty, or at a lavish expense-account lunch, or in a quick visit that amounts to little more than a hello and handshake.

When Hinman and Burfine went all over the country to call on major customers, they spent hours at each customer's location finding out how they could make their teleconferencing equipment to suit a variety of teleconferencing needs. They learned from lead customers exactly how to configure their new product. They had consummate customer empathy.

Such in-depth, on-site dialogue can sometimes do more than nail down the exact features of your new product. It might lead to a nugget of information that could spawn a whole new product category for your company. That's exactly what happened when the marketing director of a computer-table manufacturer visited one of his major customers. Bob Beck, marketing director of Vecta, had just spent three hours talking to MCI's facility director in Los Angeles about how she configured their computer training rooms. As he was leaving, he offhandedly asked, "What other problems do you have in your training rooms?" Her answer was completely unexpected. Seating—not the placement of the tables—was her biggest problem. Here's how he recalls that conversation:

> We had been talking about power and data, and I had been so focused on data distribution to all the tables in the room I hadn't even brought up seating. I said, "Well, tell me." She said, "It used to

be that in the training rooms we had stacking chairs, but when you are at a computer eight hours a day, they are not comfortable. It doesn't matter if you are at a desk or in a training room, you need ergonomic chairs." I asked her what she was doing about it, and she said she was buying new chairs for people at workstations, and as she was replacing them, she had their old chairs reupholstered to use in the computer training room. So I said, "What's the problem?" She said that three or four times a year she broke down the computer training room for a big meeting, and she didn't know what to do with fifty great big office chairs.

The next day back in the office Beck passed on the customer's seating problem to two designers. A month later he had a sketch of a chair with a seat that flipped up and down. A major new category of seating was born—stackable, wheeled, ergonomic chairs, called "Kart" chairs. In the first year of production, Vecta sold more than 24,000 Kart chairs, earning back the total investment spent in development and marketing in twelve months. To date, more than 75,000 Kart chairs have been sold and are in training rooms all across America, with an average wholesale price of $300 each. They have won ten design awards.

Beck, Hinman, Burfine, and scores of other blockbuster team members visited customers where their products might be used, and looked and listened. What are the questions to ask when you visit your customers? Here's a four-pack of suggestions:[2]

1. What can't you do that you would like to do?

2. If you could change one thing about the product you are now using, what would it be?

3. Are there any tasks you would like to do with the
   product you are now using that you can't?

4. What does this product not do that it should do?

The answers will probably elicit insights you wouldn't get otherwise. These up-close-and-personal interviews allow you and your
team to make more informed decisions about the product you are
creating, giving you an advantage no outside consultant's marketing
report can. What can you achieve with *go, look,* and *listen?*

- You identify unmet customer needs.

- You may uncover new opportunities.

- You hear firsthand the likes and dislikes about a
  product or service.

- You see how customers perceive a bundle of features.

- You learn how the customer will use the product.

- You understand what goes into making a purchase
  decision.

- You may generate alternative solutions to a design.

Whenever possible, have the people who will actually be designing the product visit the customer, not just the marketing/sales
force. The designers/engineers then get the straight story without
the filter of the sales force and marketing team. Why does it make a
difference? Think of the children's game Telephone. Someone says
something to the person sitting next to him, and then he tells it to
the next person, and so on down the line. By the time it gets to the
last person, the original statement is jumbled.

In business, it's no different. When a customer's complaints or needs get translated back to the engineer through the filter of a sales or marketing person, they may possibly be quite different from what the customer actually meant. We found that on blockbuster teams the designers were the ones who often heard for themselves both what was wrong with the current prototype, as well as what was good about it, and what the end users wanted in a new product. Hinman, for instance, was not only the CEO, but also the lead technical guru on the SoundStation, and he himself visited Intel. He heard first-hand what was wrong with the current prototype, and how it could be improved.

If you feel the need to use focus groups, send your designers/ engineers to observe a variety of them. When the engineering chief at Iomega didn't believe the consultant's report, based on focus groups, that the Zip Drive needed to be redesigned, he and one of his top engineers observed a couple of focus groups themselves to hear what the people didn't like about the current con-figuration of the product. Only then did they believe what the consultants recommended. We need to point out that the focus groups for the Zip Drive were hands-on—that is, people were actually building what they wanted the model to look like with foam cubes and strips—and we believe that is why these proved constructive.

However, focus groups are not the best way to glean insights about your customers. "You can sit down and do focus groups all day long, and the majority of people in them are worthless because they just kind of sit and nod and say 'Uh-huh, uh-huh,'" Hinman observes. Other blockbuster team leaders agree—that too often people in them are reluctant to speak their mind and can't articulate what they want in a product they don't yet have. Our advice: If you want a blockbuster, rely more on interviews and observations at the customer's location and less on traditional focus groups or surveys.

We are not the first to suggest this method—go, look, and listen—for learning what customers need and want,[3] but we cannot stress it enough. The basic premise is: You spend time with multiple customers at their locations. If possible, you watch them work. You observe how they use current products or your prototype, and you listen to their needs and wants. Then you go home and do something about it.

KNOWING THE COMPETITION

Whichever way you choose to achieve consummate customer empathy, it is only half the story when creating Project Pillars. You must also know the competition. By this we mean, *know the competition inside and out.* Buy their products, study them, use them, take them apart. You are looking for the answers to four questions:

1. Does any product already on the market solve the existing problem?

2. Does your concept do it better?

3. What are the advantages/disadvantages of competitive products?

4. What do customers like or dislike about them?

Let's go back to Polycom's Brian Hinman. (We like his story because he did so many things right.) He was eminently familiar with the competition because his old company, PictureTel, *was* much of the competition. And the NEC VoicePoint product he planned to compete with was the very equipment he was using himself. When an IBM team was given the task of developing a PC that could beat Apple, one of their first to-dos was to purchase an Apple for each member of the team. "We looked at the way they were sold, we looked at the software, we wanted to see how easy they were to use," remembers the team's head of strategic planning, Larry Rohas. They took the Apples apart and put them back together again. They knew what they were up against.

DEFINING THE PILLARS

Project Pillars can be remarkably simple, as they were on the IBM PC (beat Apple; do it in twelve months). Or they may be more detailed, but either way, it should be the job of the new product development team to figure out how to achieve them. Accomplishing this usually requires a multifunctional team, so that no aspect of the new product program is ignored. Marketing does the customer and competitive analysis detailing competing products strengths and weaknesses, their growth rates, and market shares, as well as estimating the expected market for the new product. Engineering/R&D considers the advantages and disadvantages of every competing product, how their new product might be used, what features must be included, and which are nice but unnecessary. Manufacturing reviews available products to understand their costs, production problems, and limitations.

This fact-finding and defining stage shouldn't go on indefinitely. We're talking weeks versus months. We found that several of the most successful teams took from two to six weeks to define their Project Pillars. If you can't develop them within a short period of time (unless you are working on a radically new breakthrough product), you probably never will, and it is probably better to put the project on a back burner. Although we have no steadfast rule, we found that the earlier the Project Pillars are set the better. It took only two weeks for the IBM task force to formulate the Pillars for the PC. "It was probably the most creative two weeks I have ever been a part of anywhere," says Bill Lowe, the initial team director.

But still—there's always a "but" in business as well as life—sometimes the team finds that they can actually surpass the goal of the Pillars. The Zip Drive team, for instance, originally set the price of $299 for the external drive and $199 for the internal one, but found that once they hit their Pillars, they were able to reduce it even more—when it came out, the external drive sold for $199.

BEWARE HUBRIS

Sometimes even the best companies and most experienced managers trust their assumptions and fail to check them in the current environment. The technology may have advanced, customer preferences may have changed or regulations may have altered the landscape. Somebody needs to verify these. Frequently they don't; why? Hubris. The dictionary defines *hubris* as excessive pride or self-confidence, something the Greeks knew all too well. Hubris was their downfall. They were always going off to battle half-cocked, blithely ignoring the warning signs, because they thought they were invincible.

The same happens in business, and it happens a lot more than companies like to admit. Why does it go on? Who could be that naive? The quick answer is, just about everyone: from the CEO to the technician; anyone whose past success has led him to believe that he is invincible. He thinks he knows the market, its needs, and what the customer wants better than the customer himself. And so hubris overtakes common sense. Riding on the wings of past glories, supremely self-confident managers charge ill prepared into battle without the intelligence needed, such as listening to customers or thoroughly analyzing the competition.

Hubris was certainly among the problems associated with the ill-fated PC jr. at IBM. Gary Pitt, engineering manager on the PC jr., explains:

> We were so caught up in the growth that we were experiencing, the success of the PC, that there was a kind of euphoria—a sense that anything we tried would be successful. We just did not pay enough attention to the vision or the market for the PC jr. We had a planning manager, and we did some work identifying the market, but we didn't understand the importance of the jr. being compatible with the PC. We were trying to design a product for the home market without really understanding what that meant, what people would use it for in the home. We concentrated on games, and on providing attachments to the TV, and reducing costs. And so we sacrificed compatibility with the regular PC and that doomed it to failure.

If it could happen at IBM, it could happen to you. If you ever feel yourself falling into this trap, remind yourself. Arrogance begets hubris begets failure.

Project Pillars are not quite everything to creating a block-buster—but they are at least a first critical step on the road. Fail here, and your chances of creating a blockbuster go down dramatically, for your Project Pillars have tremendous downstream consequences for the success or failure of a project.

It's not easy coming up with a great idea, but if you immerse yourself in your customers' environment, you'll be more likely to have that *eureka!* moment that leads to the next blockbuster. You go, you look, you listen. You scope out the competition. You stay humble. That's how blockbuster ideas take root.

⑥ Lickety Stick Improvisation

Nailing Process with the PowerShot Staple Gun

So now you have the foundation for a blockbuster: senior management is closely aligned with the new product development—in fact, senior management is likely to have come up with the Project Pillars. You're now ready to move forward and actually turn the concept into a reality.

How do blockbuster teams do that? Blockbuster practice number three: Improvise "Lickety Stick." Go from concept to prototype to market test to next prototype to market test to next prototype *lickety split* until the product "sticks" with the customer. Each iteration doesn't have to be perfect; it just has to be better than the last one. We call the process *Lickety Stick*.

Implementing Lickety Stick was how Polycom made their first big sale when they showed the Gumby prototype to Intel. Although Gumby was far from perfect, it was close enough to elicit customer feedback and suggestions. Iomega also quickly iterated with the design of the Zip Drive until they got it just right. Other blockbuster teams you'll read about did this too.

Lickety Stick differs from the accepted norm today. Conventional wisdom dictates that NPD teams complete a multiphase/multigate process (idea generation, screening and evaluation, development, testing, launch) in an orderly, sequential fashion. At the end of each phase, companies conduct a review meeting at which the core team and senior management make a decision about whether or not to move on to the next phase or kill it. At each review, the possibility exists that the project might be dropped completely, or recycled back to the previous stage for further refining.

Percentage of Teams Completing NPD Phases Proficiently

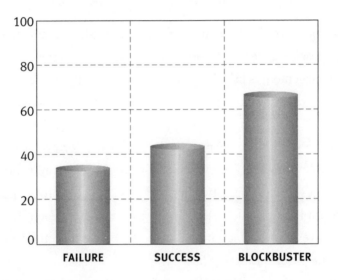

FIGURE 6.1

Blockbuster NPD teams were twice as likely as failed teams to complete the development and launch phases proficiently and one and one-half times more likely to do them well than successful teams.

However, when we analyzed our data, we found that although the blockbuster teams were completing the standard five phases of product development like other teams (see Figure 6.1), they were not going through the "gates." Instead of completing one phase and conducting for a go/kill decision at a review meeting, they kept moving forward, talking to customers and trying to sell an early concept of the product by showing them the current prototype, while R&D was still working feverishly to finalize the specs—and improvising quickly to turn out yet another iteration of the product. (See Figure 6.2.)

Percentage of Teams That Improvised Proficiently

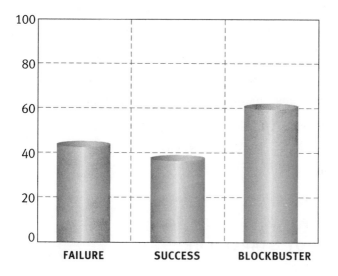

FIGURE 6.2

Blockbuster NPD teams were over one and one-half times more likely than successful teams to be proficient at improvising Lickety Stick, rather than by following a rigid plan. One of the ways that teams improvised was with rapid prototyping. A quirk in our findings is that more of the failed teams improvised than the moderately successful-but-not-blockbuster teams (the middle group in our survey). Obviously, success depends on more than just improvising. Blockbuster success depends on implementing the other four practices as well.

Blockbuster teams exhibited several differences from the norm of conventional NPD approach. First, the time sequence was markedly compressed; second, the team frequently went back to the drawing board—if the prototype failed to garner customer enthusiasm, the team repeatedly reworked the design—and third, most striking of all was that the blockbuster teams seldom if ever went through time-consuming phase reviews. Where the traditional process is more like a series of tollgates on the thruway, a pay-as-you-go process, the blockbuster teams acted as if they had an automated E-ZPass attached to their project's dashboard. There was never any discussion about whether the project should be killed—the decision to proceed was a foregone conclusion. The issue was not go versus kill, but rather GO, GO, GO! This doesn't mean blockbuster teams weren't diligent in tracking the project as it progressed. The opposite turned out to be true. Though they proceeded speedily, blockbuster teams were more likely to monitor their projects' progress and costs throughout development much more so than moderately successful or failed teams. (See Figure 6.3.)

Let's see how Lickety Stick works in action. Then we will discuss each component in more detail.

NAILING PROCESS WITH THE POWERSHOT STAPLE GUN

Back in the 1970s when Marimekko prints stapled to wood frames were popular wall hangings, teenager Mike Marks spent his after-school hours at a furniture store stapling the fabric to the frames. The trouble was, the staple gun he used—the silver Arrow T-50—was extremely hard to operate. "You really needed three hands to use the thing," he says, "one to hold the fabric, one to squeeze the

Percentage of Teams
That Tracked Their Progress Effectively

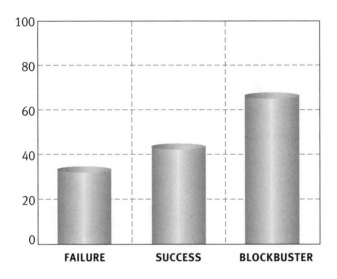

FIGURE 6.3

Blockbuster teams were more than twice as likely than the unsuccessful teams to track their projects' progress and costs often and regularly, and almost a third more likely than the moderately successful teams.

handle, and one to hold down the front of the tool." Frequently the front of the stapler bounced up and the staples didn't go all the way into the wood. Besides being inefficient, firing the stapler required a lot of strength. After firing it ten times or so, he had to rest.

Marks thought the staple gun was ineffective—you had to push on the back and the staple came out the front, the opposite of how a desk stapler worked, where you press down on the front and the staple comes out the front.

Fast-forward nearly two decades. Mike is a partner with his brother, Joel, and a college buddy, Brad Golstein, in a company called

The Arrow T-50 staple gun design has remained unchanged for nearly half a century. Arrow T-50 is a registered trademark of Arrow Fastener Company. Photo courtesy of Mike Marks.

WorkTools. Their little company had one product, the Squeeze-Driver, a screwdriver that you squeezed instead of rotated. It was a good idea—it had tested well with consumers and retailers, and they had considerable success promoting it—but once battery-powered screwdrivers hit the market, the SqueezeDriver became obsolete. "We were spent emotionally and broken financially," says Mike.

Their company needed a new product. The three of them were casting about for a new idea over Thanksgiving weekend in 1990 at the home where Joel and Mike grew up in Westwood, California, when Mike came across his old Arrow T-50 staple gun, and he remembered how poorly it worked. Could they improve on it? he wanted to know. Could they make an effective stapler so easy to handle their mother could use it?

After listening to Mike's complaints about the stapler, Joel realized that it was made backward. Why was the user pushing on the back when the staple came out the front? And did it have to be so hard to fire? During the next few weeks, Joel designed a better one.

Joel is not your everyday inventor. A former aeronautical engineer at TRW, he's designed equipment that ended up orbiting on satellites. As a teenager, he outfitted the spare room above the garage with everything from running water to illegal cable TV. Like all true inventors, he has his own style when he begins working on a new idea. He doesn't sit down at a drafting table or a computer. Instead, he finds a quiet place where he will not be disturbed. He shuts the door, gets comfortable, and closes his eyes. Then the real work begins. "I actually imagine that the tool I'm thinking about is in my hand," he says. "I envision its balance, which fingers I use, what are the contours of the stapler, what does the handle do, how far does it go. I mentally push it against paper or wood, and fire it. Then I start to get an idea of the shape of it." Only later does he sketch out his vision.

Joel's initial drawing was crude, but it captured the essence of a new concept in staple guns—it had a forward-action mechanism, which meant that you pressed on the front and presto! the staple came out the front. Now he had to make a working model. A couple of months later, after trying various mechanisms and materials, he succeeded. The one that worked was made out of sheet metal. It was complete with springs and a feed mechanism. Its forward-action design not only made the stapler much easier to fire than conventional models, but also allowed the staples to be driven flat and flush, the way they were supposed to be.

Mike, the marketing guru in their small company, took the working prototype, along with an Arrow T-50 staple gun, to a local

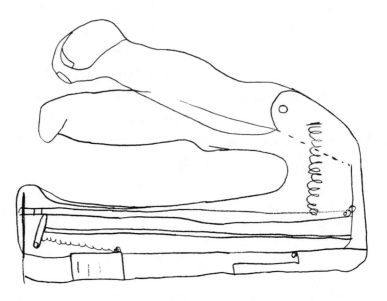

The first sketch of what would become the PowerShot stapler. You push the handle down and the staple shoots out the same end. Illustration courtesy of WorkTools, Inc.

lumberyard and set up a table. He asked customers to try both staplers and answer a few questions. If they would take his one-page survey, he'd give them a free drill chuck. Sixty-five people took him up on his offer. WorkTools' new stapler got an overwhelming positive response. All but one preferred the prototype to the Arrow. Mike knew he had something and the new staple gun was on its way.

He was hopeful but cautious. WorkTools had been stung before with the SqueezeDriver. Yes, people had liked that one when they tried it in market tests against a regular screwdriver; and yes, it had received a fair amount of promotion on everything from QVC to the cover of the Brookstone catalog. It had even won a few design awards. But still it fizzled in the marketplace because Marks had not done a head-to-head customer survey comparing it with a battery-operated screwdriver. He admits that if he had, the results of his testing probably would have been quite different. The battery-operated screwdriver would turn out to be the real competition—and it had a national advertising campaign behind it.

The wax mold Joel Marks quickly built to produce the first PowerShot prototype.
Photo courtesy of WorkTools, Inc.

Marks says SqueezeDriver netted the three of them little more than minimum wage, but claims their unfortunate experience taught them several valuable lessons: First, it taught them the value of testing their product with the customer head-to-head with other products; and second, how to analyze survey responses when trying out a new product. They learned the subtle differences in intensity from potential customers.

The first PowerShot stapler prototype that Mike Marks took to the lumberyard for the head-to-head test against the Arrow T-50.
Photo courtesy of WorkTools, Inc.

IN SEARCH OF THE ELUSIVE *HOT YES!*

If the reaction to your idea from potential customers is "Interesting idea," that's one thing. If however, they say, "Where can I buy it?" that's another. Listen to how Mike Marks differentiates between a lukewarm response and one that means you have a winner.

If less than fifty percent of the people prefer the new design, I would discard the idea. If it's fifty percent or better, I'd take a look at it. If the number is eighty to ninety percent who say they like the new product, that's something worth taking a serious look at. With another product [an adjustable hanger], we got a ninety percent preference response from the people we showed it to, but it turned out the "yeses" were not what I would call *hot yeses!* A *hot yes!* is that they want to buy this new product now. With a hot yes! they don't say "I like it better." They say, "I like it better and I'll buy it now." My feeling is that you need at least above fifty percent *hot yeses!* or more for a hit. Sometimes it's hard to ask if they would buy it—so much depends on the quality of your prototype. People see what you're showing as the reality of what the final product will be.

One way of getting the hot yes percentage is to ask if people are willing to pay a higher price for your product than the current market leader. For example, the Arrow stapler was available for $15, and I'd ask, "Would you buy ours for $20?" If they said, "Yes" and "I would buy it right now"—that's the hottest yes. And I think that you need approximately thirty percent of these responses for a slam dunk.

Mike did not pull these cutoff points out of the air. When WorkTools test-marketed the SqueezeDriver, they got 50 percent hot yeses! Without a national advertising campaign to stimulate demand, he says, the 50 percent turned out to be not nearly good enough. For a one-product company, the product must jump off the shelves to be a success. "Despite the fact that I was absolutely clear in my head that there was a market for this new stapler," Mike cautions, "I would never rely only on my own opinion." Not after the SqueezeDriver fiasco.

Over the next year, Joel kept refining the design, and Mike and partner Brad Golstein, who handles the administrative and financial matters for WorkTools, would repeatedly try out the prototypes themselves and with potential users, always seeking answers to Joel's questions: *How did the handle grip feel? Was the pressure to shoot the thing about right? Too hard? Was the staple gun balanced so it was easy to maneuver?* Half fooling around, they would shoot the staples into the air to see how far they would travel, and compare the distances with those of competitive products. The distance gave them some idea of its power. Joel would listen to customer comments, then go back and work on the design some more. Not every prototype was a keeper. One of the keys to creating a good design is being willing to throw something away, even though you may have worked on for months. "I've gotten very good at remaining unemotional toward a design, because even dead-end models almost always have some lesson for the future," Joel says.

He was still tinkering with his design the following August when all three of them attended the National Hardware Show in Chicago. There they learned about the market for staple guns: size, distribution, who was having success with them, who wasn't, and how much was spent on advertising. From information gained from the show, they correctly estimated that market to be around $200 million.

The WorkTools trio was at a crossroads—should they try to manufacture and market the staple gun themselves? They had applied for the necessary patents to do so. Yet they weren't averse to licensing it to a well-established brand. At the hardware show they learned that Black and Decker seemed to be in the business, though just barely, with a market share of less than 1 percent. Mike remembers that the Black and Decker staplers were poorly made and manufactured by an outside contractor, and simply had Black and Decker's name slapped on them. A better stapler might be of interest to them.

Now getting a big company interested in your design is a tricky matter. If you just call them up outright, you will probably be shuffled through a bureaucratic maze. So Mike approached them by saying that he wanted to buy some parts for the SqueezeDriver, and once he was in the system with someone he could talk to, Mike switched gears: You know, we've got something you might be interested in looking at. . . .

The timing couldn't have been better. Black and Decker had just put together a development team that was looking for a better stapler. Joel remembers well their first meeting. Of course the Black and Decker people were calling the shots—they were the guys from the big company, after all, and the meeting was on their turf. But once Joel pulled out the prototype and gave the Black and Decker people something to see, touch, and play with, the mood in the room shifted, Joel remembers. Now the authority shifted to the WorkTools trio. "It turns out Black and Decker had tried to build a forward-action staple gun themselves about five years before that," Joel says, "but whoever did it didn't have any understanding of mechanics, because the thing looked like it weighed fifty pounds." The superiority of the WorkTools prototype was apparent to all. Making a decent working prototype had been a lot of trouble. The prototype had gone through multiple iterations, but without doing so, the WorkTools trio knew they would have had a hard time piquing Black and Decker's interest.

Many more meetings would follow before Black and Decker signed up to sell the product. For one of those meetings, Joel built yet another new prototype, but it cracked just before Mike left for the airport. Joel quickly brazed the broken lever back on and warned his brother, "I can't guarantee it will be good for more than one firing, but it *should* last through the meeting." It actually survived two presentations, but broke in the middle of the third. Not perfect by any means, but good enough: the Black and Decker team gave the green light to licensing the WorkTools stapler.

The final PowerShot stapler with its forward action design created a new standard for staple guns. Photo courtesy of WorkTools, Inc.

Once that happened, Black and Decker set some deadlines. They wanted to bring out the new stapler in a year. Joel kept on improving different parts of the stapler—even as some parts were being tooled for production, he continued to tweak the design until the window for further changes slammed shut.

The forward-action stapler, christened the PowerShot, was launched on schedule in 1993. And, in the first eighteen months of sales, Black and Decker's share of the staple gun market rocketed from virtually zero to almost 20 percent.[1] Since then, the PowerShot family of staplers has sold approximately six million units in under eight years, and enjoys continuing annual growth in sales. The PowerShot Tool Company was born a few years later when a former B&D sales manager bought Black and Decker's staple gun division. Sears Roebuck has also licensed the design, and sells the EasyFire stapler under their Craftsman label.

The PowerShot was a significant improvement in design, creating a new standard for staplers. Easy to hold and easy to use, it has been heralded as one of the best and most innovative designs of the 1990s. *Popular Mechanics* gave it their 1994 Design Engineering Award and *BusinessWeek*, in conjunction with the Industrial Design Society of America, awarded it two gold medals.

LICKETY STICK RULE #1:
Get that first prototype out the door—*fast!*

The PowerShot story illustrates one overreaching principle of Lickety Stick: Get that first prototype out the door quickly! The initial prototype—no matter how crude—is for customer feedback at the beginning of the development process, not near the end, unlike what happens in the typical NPD phase-review process.

What kind of time frame are we talking about? Depending on the product, think weeks, not months. If the product is technologically a real stretch, think two months, not six. Use off-the-shelf components if possible and if it will accelerate the time to first prototype.

The data gleaned from testing a real product with potential customers can be priceless—and impossible to get any other way. Designers can learn early on what the project's flaws are, and what they need to do to build a better one. When the WorkTools trio took a prototype of the forward-action stapler to their first meeting with Black and Decker, it had already been successfully test-marketed with consumers. They came to the table with bragging rights about their terrific new product.

Other blockbuster teams followed the same formula. Motorola created a series of different types of prototypes, moving from sketches to cardboard to Styrofoam models of what would become the wildly successful StarTAC cell phone. By the end of the first year of development, 1993, they had made more than twenty prototypes. Their first working models weighed a hefty two pounds. Given to congressmen in Washington, D.C., to test, it was quickly nicknamed "the Brick." Congressmen complained that they couldn't hold it for more than five minutes without their hands getting tired. Obviously, it had to be a whole lot lighter. Today the StarTAC is the size of a small wallet and weighs approximately three ounces. But though the Brick was heavy, it confirmed for Motorola that they were onto something big: when time came for the congressmen to return their cell phones, many of them refused until they were promised a newer model. Motorola knew they had a winner—a *hot yes!*

The Ulrich brothers had their first prototype of an adult

scooter in the hands of family and friends *in less than two weeks* after Karl's initial email to the designer—his brother, Nathan. While it is not a technically complex invention, and Nathan happens to have a machine shop, he didn't put the idea aside and delay. If he had, it's likely someone else would have beat them to market, because kids' scooters were becoming a hot category at the time. "We produced it [a working model] very early and people rode it and said, this is really cool," Karl says. They figured that the worst-case scenario was that they would sell a thousand of the scooters to their friends. "Or it could be a whole new category," Karl adds, which is exactly what happened.

That early prototype was undoubtedly instrumental in getting an award-winning design firm, Lunar Designs, on board to work on the final specifications. "Absent that prototype," Karl contends, "we would have had a harder time convincing them, because with just a sketch, they look at you and say, what's so good about that? There's so much uncertainty about the marketplace that the value of trying it out is extremely high, relative to the cost it would take you to survey and analyze, and try to predict what will happen."

Brian Hinman of Polycom says that prototyping allows you to readily see where you are off base with your new product, and correct the glitches well before manufacturing. "The biggest mistake entrepreneurs make is to get all religious about their stuff, and hold up a new product for two years thinking about it, thinking that it is going to be the greatest thing ever created," he observes. "More than likely, the harsh realities will set in when you get your first reactions from the marketplace, but if you had done your research with a prototype as you went along, you would not be so far off base."

LICKETY STICK RULE #2:
Now Do It Again . . . and Again

The next step in Lickety Stick is bringing out subsequent iterations as quickly as possible—bang, bang, bang. It means showing each prototype to end users from different market segments, and refining it, but still keeping your Project Pillars firm. It is okay to adjust product specifications, but do not remake the project to meet every customer's whim. Polycom got some very specific suggestions on how to make their teleconferencing equipment appeal to different market segments, but never veered from their Project Pillars. The same was true with other blockbuster teams. Kim Edwards of Iomega remembers that period of development as "ordered chaos":

Lickety Stick rule #2 in action—build multiple prototypes quickly. Iomega produced a variety of models before deciding on the final Zip Drive design. Photo courtesy of Iomega.

We never knew what the customer was going to say, and we had some rude awakenings along the way. It is like driving down a railroad track, and you have a crew building the track fifty feet in front of the train. You don't know the direction that the track is going to take. You might think it's going to veer left, but it goes straight instead.

You can't ferret out this kind of data any other way. Not only does prototyping make the final product more technologically polished; it also can inspire commitment from both inside the company, and outside as well, with venture capitalists, suppliers, and customers. It validates that the idea is viable and not just a theoretical concept.[2]

SPIRAL DEVELOPMENT AT
THE DEPARTMENT OF DEFENSE

The Lickety Stick process is similar to what is called Spiral Development at the Department of Defense. Customers—soldiers—are at the center of this process, for they help design successive improvements rapidly, providing immediate feedback to onsite contractors. Taking their cues from soldiers' comments, the contractors come back again and again with a series of prototypes that the contractor, the scientist, and the soldier/customer assess once more.

In the development of the Unmanned Aerial Vehicle (UAV), the kind of aircraft used in Afghanistan, prototypes delivered clear views of the battlefield to ground commanders. However, when tested in mock battle, the UAV pictures were fuzzy above 6,000 feet, and could be shot down. The problem was solved by a soldier watching the testing who suggested simply putting two lenses together to extend the range to 12,000 feet. His good idea became the quick solution.

GAMMA TESTING

If a prototype is viable, you actually might be able to sell it—well before you go into production. Making a sale based on a prototype, known as Gamma testing,[3] lets companies know early on what kind of reception their new product is likely to receive. Also, when customers are willing to "sign on the dotted line" you will have a much clearer picture of whether the product is good or bad, versus merely asking them in a survey or focus group if they like the concept. For example, Searle solicited and received orders for NutraSweet well before the sugar substitute had government approval and was being manufactured. Likewise, Polycom had an order for six hundred SoundStations from Intel prior to having perfected the design.

After the Zip 100 was launched, customers expressed interest in a smaller drive with higher capacity. So Iomega launched the Zip 250.

Photo courtesy of Iomega.

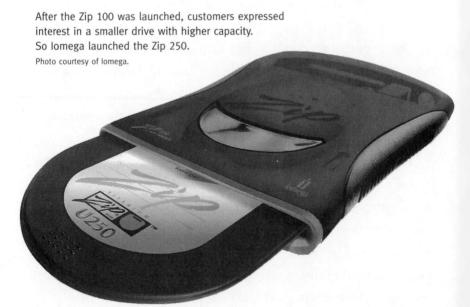

We're not the only ones to suggest rapid prototyping before launch.[4] However, where Lickety Stick differs is that it incorporates both an early-to-market prototype, as well as the rapid iterations that follow. Also, Lickety Stick does not end with launch. After launch, there will be opportunities to improve the product. The trick is to do it quickly.

EVOLUTIONARY VERSUS INCREMENTAL NEW PRODUCTS

Not all products, however, need to use the Lickety Stick approach to the same extent. If your new product represents a small incremental change, rule #1 is likely not necessary, as the products already available are, in a sense, your market tests. But rule #2 still applies and companies should resist the temptation to rest on their laurels. They should continue to modify and improve their products. For other products that make a big evolutionary leap forward, such as the Zip Drive, the SoundStation, and many other blockbusters we studied, testing with prototypes is imperative. If you are entering a market where there is uncertainty in either the market or technology, the feedback from early and rapid prototyping can be critical to your success.

If you are wondering how to tell the difference between a new product that is an incremental improvement and an evolutionary advance, ask yourself these questions:

- Does the new product represent a major difference from competitors' in the way it is used, or how it functions?

- Do you expect the new product to create a new market category?

- Does the new product use some technology that is
  unproven or uncertain?

If the answer to any of these questions is yes, your new product
will probably benefit from using Lickety Stick. If the answer is no to all
of them, you probably do not need to implement Lickety Stick; the
normal phase-review process is likely a better choice for your team.

FROM REALITY TO VIRTUAL

Although Polycom, WorkTools, and several other blockbuster teams
we studied relied on physical prototypes, many teams used virtual
prototypes as well as tangible ones. When we first began our study a
decade ago, the technology for computer representations (virtual
prototypes) was not as readily available or as cost effective as it is
today. But that's changed. Virtual prototyping is common and will
become more so in the future. In the automobile industry, for example, car manufacturers can show customers the car desired—color
and appointments—without them ever stepping inside one. In some
cases, it's even possible to see how something might work virtually
and "try it out," such as a new bicycle pump.[5] With the cost of a computer modeling and imaging coming down, even small start-ups with
modest budgets can demonstrate to potential customers how their
new product will look and work—virtually.

But, a word of caution. In many situations, a virtual prototype
will not elicit the same insights from the customer as a tangible one.
Although virtual prototypes can provide rich information, whenever
possible and feasible, get a physical prototype into customers' hands.
"Until you put a specific [tangible] product in front of potential customers, and set a price, and really threaten to sell it to them—that's

when you come away with pearls of wisdom," observes engineering director John Mailhot, whose team at Lucent developed the blockbuster WaveStar Digital Video, a system for transmitting high-definition video signals over the air.*

LICKETY STICK RULE #3:
A Hard Deadline

One more critical component to the Lickety Stick process is a hard deadline, held over the heads of the NPD team like the sword of Damocles. This created a sense of urgency that drove the blockbuster teams to their great successes. The deadline could be one of several types—the next annual trade show, a contract to fill, the impending collapse of a company unless the next product saves it, or a team's sense that if they don't prove themselves soon, they might lose their jobs.

Lucent, for example, was desperate to demonstrate its WaveStar technology at the 1999 National Association of Broadcasters trade show. "We knew that several of our competitors would be coming out with a revised and updated system, and we had to have something too," says Mailhot. "People build their entire engineering schedule around showing their new technology at the April show, and shipping it in June." At Iomega, CEO Edwards didn't mince words: "No Comdex, no company, no choice." Polycom also had a trade show deadline; plus they had agreed to ship products to Intel by late summer, so the pressure was on. Other teams knew they had to launch their product in time for the next Christmas season. Some were meeting a deadline set by their CEO.

---

* Lucent's WaveStar Digital Video was subsequently sold to Aastra Digital Video Systems.

At least one team knew they would lose credibility, and possibly their jobs, if they failed to meet expectations. At Kodak, the team's previous attempts to develop a throwaway camera had failed miserably, and their reputation was in the toilet—there was even talk of shutting down their entire division. The team's drive to deliver was "born out of desperation," remembers Alan Vandemoere, Kodak's manufacturing and operations manager who was on the team. In a record seven months, the team developed the FunSaver single-use camera. A runaway success, it exceeded all expectations after only three months. For each of the next seven years, FunSaver showed a growth rate of 35 to 40 percent.

Sometimes it's not just a division that's in jeopardy if a deadline isn't met—it can impact the company's entire future. Polycom only had so much rope from their venture capitalists—if the company didn't successfully deliver soon, the money would be cut off.

Polycom engineers and all the other blockbuster teams we've talked about had that inner gotta-get-this-done attitude that's seemingly impossible to replicate without a hard deadline staring you down. Hard deadlines elicit superhuman effort that wouldn't happen otherwise. Everybody on the team will say Whew! once the deadline is met, but most will take away a remembrance of a time when the intensity and sense of purpose made the long work hours enormously satisfying and strangely pleasurable.

In contrast, if you let your deadlines slip—and there will always be good reasons for allowing them to—damaging mischief can creep into your project in the form of expanding vision, diminishing enthusiasm, and losing people. The likelihood of adding unnecessary features to the new product increases. But if you have a hard deadline, the emphasis changes from what you should do to what you can do given the time constraints. Then once the first product is out, continue with Lickety Stick and constantly improve it.

At IBM, the doomed DataMaster project, the precursor to the PC, went on just short of four years, during which time the technology leap-frogged right over it and made the product out-of-date on the day it was introduced. In the next chapter, you'll read about how features were added to a new computer at Apple and how it grew and grew—and the deadline pushed forward repeatedly—until its price escalated to five times the original estimate and it became a giant fiasco for the company.

If a deadline is delayed because the product simply isn't ready— but is almost ready—we urge supreme caution. It may be tempting to let a launch date slip by, but almost always you need to resist this. The product will rarely be perfect—it will only be late to market. Like everything else in life, there are exceptions to this rule. Pharmaceuticals, some Defense Department programs, and radical innovations have their own timetables, and can be developed and launched only when the product is truly ready. But for incremental and evolutionary new products a concrete deadline set at the beginning has tremendous implications, and should not be ignored.

LICKETY STICK RULE #4:
Search for the Hot Yes!

What you are searching for with your prototypes is the "hot yes!" that we talked about earlier. What percentage of them do you need? That depends on who you are. As we said, a small company like WorkTools was looking for at least a 50 percent hot-yes! rate. An established brand-name company with deep pockets does not need such a high number. Former Chrysler vice chairman Robert Lutz describes the hot yeses he got when he tested the redesign of the Dodge Ram pickup in 1994. He recalls:

When we showed the early prototype for the new "big-rig inspired Dodge Ram pickup" to customer focus groups in the early 1990s, the reaction was so polarized that the room practically vibrated with magnetism. A whopping eighty percent of the respondents disliked the bold new drop fender design; a lot even hated it! They wanted their pickups to keep on resembling the horizontal corn-flake boxes they were used to—not to be striking or bold. According to traditional customer research strategy, we would have thrown that design out on its ear, or at least toned it down to placate the hatemongers, but that would have been looking through the wrong end of the telescope. The remaining twenty percent of the clinic participants were truly, madly in love with the design, and since the old Ram had only had about four percent of the market at the time, we figured, What the hell, even if only half of those positive respondents actually buy it, that will more than double our market share. The result—our share of the pickup market shot up twenty percent on the radical new design.[6]

The Ram pickup went on to be a huge success for Chrysler—with only 20 percent hot yeses! As we said, the percentage you need depends on the size of your company, the familiarity of the brand and the amount of national advertising you will devote to the product.

LICKETY STICK IS NOT THE ANSWER FOR EVERY NPD

Lickety Stick doesn't work all the time in all situations, a topic we'll take up in Chapter 9. If your phase-review process produces blockbusters—great! Stick with it. But if your company has not produced a blockbuster recently, consider using the Lickety Stick process for one project. Compare the results with the more traditional NPD method that your company usually follows. We believe you will be pleased with the results—as long as you combine it with the other four practices. It has worked for many others with amazing results.

(7) Information Exchange

Creating a Knowledge Core at Apple

In a typical new product development effort, team members can understandably be reluctant to freely share their ideas and information. Why? Because if engineering openly tells marketing about their latest and greatest ideas, marketing will use them to make promises to customers. Then engineering has to try to deliver. If that engineer hadn't opened his mouth in the first place, they wouldn't be in this fix. Marketing is also cautious because if they tell engineering about the promises made, engineering will be similarly dismayed. Therein lies the conflict, a conflict that can derail any new product effort.

But when we asked blockbuster team members how they handled communication across disciplines, it turned out this wasn't a problem at all. They readily shared information. (See Figure 7.1.) In contrast, on NPD teams that failed, not only was communication sparse, but it was even discouraged! Cross-functional team meetings would be canceled and not rescheduled. And when they were held, one member of an unsuccessful team told us: "It felt like an exercise in who wasn't listening to whom."

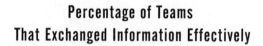

Percentage of Teams
That Exchanged Information Effectively

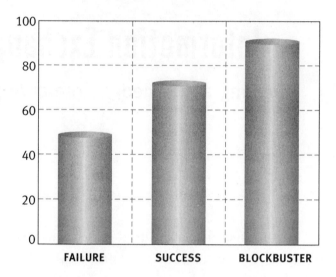

FIGURE 7.1

Blockbuster teams were almost twice as likely as failures to have effective ways of sharing information, and almost a third more likely than the moderately successful teams. Over 91 percent of the blockbusters scored themselves outstanding in knowledge exchange, compared to 72 percent of the moderately successful teams, and only 49 percent of the failed teams.

The difference between how good information exchange can strengthen your NPD and how poor communication can foil it is best demonstrated with the story of two teams at Apple Computer. One was excellent in information exchange and produced a blockbuster, and the other wasn't and created a dog—almost taking the company down with it.

CREATING A KNOWLEDGE CORE AT APPLE

Steve Wozniak, Steve Jobs, and Ron Wayne started a computer company on April Fool's Day, 1976. Their goal was to design, produce, and sell an affordable personal computer targeted primarily to electronic home hobbyists and electronic enthusiasts. They weren't the first out there—MITS (Micro Instrumentation and Telemetry Systems) offered the first personal computer for sale in 1975. It came as a kit and appealed to the electronic enthusiast. Other companies offered crude computers for around $500.

The trio introduced their first "computer" three months later. It also was a kit with a printed circuit board that you plugged into the back of your television set. Boasting a modest four kilobytes of memory, it didn't even come with a keyboard. With a selling price of $666.66, it was one of the first computers to be mass-produced, even though the two hundred they made doesn't sound like much today. But that was back in what might be called the Stone Age of personal computers. All but twenty-five of those early models were sold.[1] Soon afterward, Wozniak and Jobs bought out Wayne, and together they formed Apple Computer. As for the name? Jobs had previously worked at an organic apple orchard, and he thought of an apple as a perfect fruit: high in nutritional value, packaged in a nice case, not easily damaged.

The following year, Wozniak worked on their next computer, designing it almost completely by himself—*for himself*. And when it did come out the following April, the Apple II was a huge leap forward: it had color graphics, a keyboard, a power supply in a distinctive beige case, and eight kilobytes of memory, all for $1,298. It appealed to many people because its operating system was easy to use, unlike the others available at the time that were too complicated for the typical user. You could play games on it. You could pop off the case and see how the thing worked. You could work on two tasks at once because it had a split-screen capability.

Apple II was a huge success for the fledgling company. More than 4,000 units were sold in the remaining nine months of 1977.[2] Within two years, the company had shipped 35,000 units.[3] By late 1981, more than 300,000 units were sold, and demand was growing. For those glorious years in Apple's checkered history, the Apple II was the most popular PC in the world. As the market for computers broadened, the Apple II found a place in the home, the classroom, and the office.

Yet Apple wasn't out there alone. By the end of the seventies, some thirty companies were making PCs for electronic hobbyists, home computer buffs, and professional/business people. You could buy a microcomputer that cost less than $200 from a company in Great Britain or an IBM system with a color screen and a printer for $6,000. The big names in the business were Wang, IBM, and Hewlett-Packard. With price tags ranging from $5,000 to $20,000, few people bought them for home use. The Apple, in contrast, was much more affordable.

Wozniak and Jobs knew their success would be a difficult act to follow. Nevertheless, they determined to make an even better computer. In doing so, they created the legendary Apple IIe, the product that secured Apple's lead in PCs for nearly a decade.

How did they do it? How did an upstart little company create such a phenomenal blockbuster? When we interviewed people who worked on the IIe, what we noticed right away was the truly outstanding way they shared information on the team. When Wozniak created the Apple II, the company had only a handful of employees working literally out of a garage, so communication was free and

This was the motherboard that went into the first Apple IIe prototype, called the Super II. It was the first time Apple created its own custom logic chip. The motherboard was provided by Steven Weyhrich, www.apple2history.org. Photograph by Daria Amato.

easy. It was as if they were in a single all-day meeting every day. By the time they developed the Apple IIe, however, the company had grown to over 2,500 employees. The initial team on the Apple IIe was around a dozen growing to thirty by launch. Now Apple Computer needed a real system for sharing information. The one they created was breathtakingly simple, yet incredibly effective.

THE WAR ROOM

Apple designated a conference room as the IIe "war room." There, everyone working on the project could find the myriad bits of information amassed on the project easily and quickly. The concept was a stroke of genius.

In the war room the status of the different functions (R&D, marketing, manufacturing) was constantly updated on handwritten notes posted on the walls. Sure, it looked untidy, but that comfortable, lived-in feeling made everyone feel welcome—not just those on the team, but also customers, suppliers, company representatives, and so on. Here's where you came to find out who was doing what, and where every aspect of the project stood at any moment. The war room was a communication conduit that embodied the "collective consciousness" of the project. Mike Connor, the IIe project leader explains:

> The walls of the room were covered with information, ideas, input, et cetera, as well as product launch plans from everybody [both on and off the team]. So what we would do as a team is we would grab a group of sales people and bring them to the room and say, "What do you think? What needs to go in the product? What doesn't need to go in the product? What about this approach to pricing?" We took engineers, technical documentation staff, trainers, service support people—even the executives came to the room. And we didn't just bring somebody into the room once. When Apple's president Mike Markkula came through—he was really big on total quality—he pinned this little velvet pouch for an expensive bottle of scotch to the wall, and said, "When you think about quality I want you to think about this. When you think about the impact that this product is going to have on someone, I want you to think about this pouch—touch it, look at it, feel it, see the gold cords on it, enjoy the nice experience that comes from touching it—that's the experience I want someone to have with this product."

Some days the key people on the team spent whole days in the war room, as others streamed in and out with updates, bringing their concerns, criticisms, and suggestions. The whole team met there once a week. Any significant change on the project filtered out of there within minutes, so that the different functional areas knew instantly if they needed to make an adjustment.

Record Keeping in the War Room

The war room was more than a place to meet. It was also a repository of hard data, a low-tech information depository or "brain" of the Apple IIe. The handwritten notes on the walls made the writer's intent instantly clear. When someone came to the war room, he was handed a pad of yellow Post-its and a Magic Marker. If the person didn't write anything down, whoever was talking to him did. "We stuck up the suggestions on index cards, Post-its, you name it," Connor says. "We also had people put their names on the three-by-five stickies—we had the whole room covered with all these notes."

One of the Project Pillars of the Apple IIe was to target families and small businesses. So up went pictures—families, kids, business-people with home offices, letters from users and dealers, information about the top-selling software for small businesses. The aim was to make the war room a visual experience: "We were communicating that it [the Apple IIe] wasn't just another product, but that it really had a spirit of its own," comments Connor. "The war room became an incredibly powerful communication tool in creating that aura, because it captured not only what needed to be done, but also the spirit of why."

Different functional areas put up their suggestions in different parts of the room, so the information was easy to locate. At one stage, manufacturing asked that the computer be built entirely with the base plate facing up because when it was turned over during production, parts would fall out and sometimes the entire unit would fall on the floor. Engineering saw the suggestion posted in the war room and responded with dispatch. The problem was quickly solved. The war room inspired the kind of communication that allowed the team to handle any issue without making a big deal over it. The war room was such an integral part of the project that Connor and his top lieutenants took a certain amount of friendly fire within the company for their reliance on it, especially after he set up a "portable war room," a huge, rolling corkboard plastered with three-by-five-inch index cards. He wheeled it to meetings, he took it to briefings with senior management if they didn't come to the war room themselves, he took it anywhere he needed to have all the information at hand.

The Apple IIe created the new standard for personal computers. Compared to the II, it had more memory, easier screen editing and a bigger screen, all for $1,395.[4]
Computer courtesy of Joel Scharf. Photograph by Daria Amato.

No one ever questioned the target goals of the new, improved Apple because the war room kept everybody on the same page.

The result of their labors? The IIe was introduced to universal rave reviews in January 1983, and it soon garnered great word-of-mouth for being highly reliable. In fact, Apple IIe had less than half the failure rate (under 5 percent) of the Apple II. All this, at precisely the time when the demand for an affordable home computer was exploding.

The company had been shipping approximately 12,000 Apple IIs a month; almost as soon as the Apple IIe was launched, they shipped *30,000 to 40,000 a month.* In December 1983 alone, the company shipped 110,000 Apple IIes, setting a sales record for that time.[5] The technology in the Apple IIe would not be outdated for *six years,* a phenomenal length of time in the world of high tech. It was the right product at the right time for the right price: a blockbuster!

One primary reason for the success of the Apple IIe was the war room—an incredibly effective method of sharing information. It facilitated the clear and rapid communication among team members and top management. It was a focal point and a gathering place. In stark contrast is what happened on another Apple project, Lisa.

ALONG CAME LISA (AND HUBRIS)

The IIe's success sowed the seeds of failure on Apple's next project, Lisa. The runaway popularity of Apple IIe had turned a bunch of hard-core geeks into corporate kings for a while, and therein lay the problem. They suffered a near-fatal attack of hubris. They became drunk with their success. People who had scoffed at the kids in the garage trying to compete with the big boys now wanted to work for them. Jobs and Wozniak hired a number of brainy folks from other computer and electronics companies, including the venerated Xerox

Palo Alto Research Center, better known as PARC. No expense was spared on their surroundings. Apple offices went from basic, cramped quarters to a place with plush carpeting and designer potted plants.

And the war room? It got prettified. A staff was hired to keep it orderly, so all the dynamic, handwritten Post-it notes and index cards were now replaced with typed notes—prepared by a typist. Big mistake. "How likely would you be to write out something in your own hand and put it up on a wall alongside neat, nicely typed index cards?" asks Connor. "Handwriting communicates more than what's just written on the page." By formalizing the process, the creative juice and energy had been squeezed out of the room.

It was as if the Apple IIe war room was a family room where you could kick back and let it all hang out, while the Lisa so-called war room was a front parlor where you entertained guests but didn't put your feet up or say anything too surprising. Not unexpectedly, that tidy conference room was no longer a place to hang out and test new ideas. It was a derided "management tool."

The Lisa program also ran into other problems that exacerbated things including competing egos imported from different companies, no hard deadline, little to no customer research, and an expanding vision. The designers got overly ambitious, and kept adding features. The initial plan had been to offer a computer with considerably more memory than the Apple IIe at a price of $2,000. Yes, it doubled the IIe memory, but also was the first commercial application of a Graphical User Interface (GUI),[6] the name of the drop-down menu on your computer that allows you to select commands with a click of the mouse. This, however, came at a price. Runaway development costs—estimated to be well over $50 million—pushed up the price out of reach of most potential customers to a whopping $9,995.

Almost from the beginning, Lisa floppcd. Sales fell woefully below forecast. The sales estimate was 50,000 in the first year, but only 11,000 were sold. The company tried to recoup the investment with less expensive models. When those efforts failed, Lisa was retired, about two years after it was introduced. Some of its features would pave the way for the Macintosh, but that was still in the future. Many things—arrogance, resources not husbanded carefully, not having firm Project Pillars, missing the deadline, as well as the collapse of an efficient manner for sharing information—contributed to the failure of Lisa.

TWO WAYS TO SHARE INFORMATION

Better methods of sharing information would have helped the Lisa team. Two such methods that were employed by blockbuster teams involve *transactive memory* and *mechanistic memory. Transactive memory*[7] occurs when people serve as the information storage medium, sharing knowledge by free and frequent personal interaction among team members—the casual hallway discussion, the quick phone call, the formal meeting. *Mechanistic memory* occurs when a mechanical system is used to store and retrieve information. This can include anything from a three-ring notebook to a Web-based intranet system. Most teams need both methods of sharing and storing knowledge. We'll take up transactive memory first.

Transactive Memory: How the Team Interacts

Think of *transactive memory* as the human collective memory of the team—knowing who knows what. When team members need data but cannot recall it themselves, or worry that their own memories are inaccurate, they can turn to each other for help. If properly done, these interpersonal transactions can provide team members with better information than any of them could recall alone.

Teams can be trained in transactive memory, and when they begin to use it, they are more productive and make fewer errors than teams who do not.[8] We are not talking about touchy-feely team-sensitivity training or conflict resolution, but about teaching people how to run meetings and keep track of who knows what. But there are ways to improve transactive memory without expensive, time-consuming training. Consider:

Are your people physically located on one floor, or one section of a floor? Or are they spread out among several floors, or buildings? Can they be brought together? Can you make it easier for them to meet face-to-face? Do you have audio and/or video conferencing facilities they can use? All of these factors impact transactive memory.

Another way that facilitates good information exchange is to bring people together who have worked with each other before. Sharing information is easier because a large part of the communications puzzle is figuring out where you can go to get the information you need. Problems and issues that arise along the way—and they always do—can be assigned quickly to the people who are most likely to solve them. If they have worked together before, team members can anticipate the actions of others, rather than simply react to them. It's like keeping members of a winning high school hockey team together. College coaches know their chances of bringing home the trophy markedly increase if they can recruit the entire front line from one school—these players know how to win by playing off each other's strengths and weaknesses. Many blockbuster teams use the same strategy.

Let's look at the team who created the Handspring Visor, a personal digital assistant. The team consisted of eight people, seven of whom had worked together before on the Palm Pilot. Their offices and cubicles were on the same floor. When Handspring president, Jeff Hawkins, needed to know something, he was likely just to walk into somebody's cubicle and say, "Hey, what's going on?" remembers marketing director Rob Haitani. They frequently went out to lunch together where they discussed—*what else?*—their new product.

But few teams are that small or fortuitously located on a restaurant row, as the Handspring team was. Cross-functional NPD teams must find other ways to open lines of communication. An excellent way to build bonds is to send people from different teams to visit the customer on site. Say the marketer and the engineer go together— they would most likely fly together to a different city, rent a car at the airport, drive to the location together, conduct the interviews, possibly even spend the night at a hotel where they have dinner together, drive back to the airport in the morning, and fly back home.[9] Almost certainly much of the time will be spent discussing the project and getting to know one another. Later on, their familiarity with one another will make sharing information easier. Disputes over design features will inevitably surface between marketing and engineering, and the people involved are more likely to resolve matters quickly if people know one another. It's a lot easier to pick up the phone and call someone in another department if the two of you already have a good working relationship. So the trip serves two purposes: not only will they learn from the customer, they will also have opened communication channels between themselves. We found that whether they become friends is not critical; what does matter is the desire and ability to readily share information, which can be enhanced by this kind of up-close-and-personal interaction.

Team Meetings: When, Why, What?

We are frequently asked how often should team meetings be held. Although no clear rule emerged from our data as to whether daily, weekly, biweekly, or monthly meetings are best, we found that most blockbuster teams usually met daily during the initial stage when they were formulating the Project Pillars. Some blockbuster teams continued to have short daily briefings throughout the entire NPD process, but most met less frequently as the project progressed. Then weekly, or even monthly, meetings were enough. Iomega CEO Kim Edwards started out having coffee with the engineers every day at the office from 7:00 to 7:30 A.M.; eventually the coffee klatch grew to include most of the team. The IBM PC team had daily morning get-togethers during the early phase of development for quick status updates to ensure that at most only one day would pass between the time an issue cropped up, and the time the entire group heard about it. But the informal meetings, engineer Dave Bradley adds, "helped generate a shared vision of what we were doing." Once the Project Pillars and plan were established, the meetings were less frequent.

Keeping the meetings brief and to the point was another hallmark of blockbuster teams. At Lucent, meetings were kept to one hour. "The more time you spend talking about something, the less time you spend doing it," explains John Mailhot, WaveStar engineering director. "There was no set agenda. We essentially went around the room asking, What are you up to? What do you need?" There may have been no formal, written-out agenda, but the meetings focused on where various team members were on their parts of the project, any issues that stood in the way of reaching those goals, and staying on schedule. At IBM, when it was rumored that the printer ribbons for the PC under development were carcinogenic, everybody working on the printer design, from engineering and manufacturing, attended the weekly meeting. (The rumor turned out to be false.) On the Apple IIe, "our meetings tended to be status oriented—what are the obstacles to what we want to do, and how can we fix them?" says the first product manager on the project, Taylor Pohlman. "They were action oriented and brief."

When should meetings be held? We found that weekly Monday mornings worked best. "You would come out of there at full velocity with a loaded revolver of things you had to get done that week," says Polycom's Jeff Rodman.

Blockbuster project leaders knew how to conduct their team meetings. The agenda frequently would be a quick review of what the team was supposed to complete the week before, how well they had achieved those goals, and what had to be done in the upcoming week—always with one eye on the Pillars.

Mechanistic Memory: Where Hard Information Is Stored

Sharing knowledge about the project through personal interaction is only half the information exchange picture. You need a good system for recording, storing, and retrieving data, a system that allows all the team members to access it at will. This is *mechanistic memory*. Consider how the Apple IIe's war room was, in fact, a repository of written suggestions and other data that team members wrote out and stuck to the walls. The room incorporated the three basic aspects of an effective mechanistic system: (1) recording (the sticky notes), (2) storing (sticky notes stuck to the wall), and (3) retrieving (the comments were easily available to all who came to the war room).

For most projects, the recording of data on many projects need not be overly complicated—in fact, sometimes the simpler the better.* A list of to-do items—*who has to do what by when*—may be adequate. The notes can be reviewed at the following meeting, and the next steps outlined. Some failed teams recorded copious minutes to meetings rather than to-do action items. Detailed minutes can be a waste of time for the scribe as well as those who are supposed to read them. What we did find crucial was that any action-item notes and decisions made during the meeting were documented, filed, and readily available. They could be tacked to the war room wall, placed in a three-ring notebook that is accessible to team members, or stored in a computer-based shared intranet system that all can use. In contrast, we found that on failed NPD teams they often did not have a good system for capturing information and critical data sometimes got lost because nobody documented it or could find it.

Although 34 percent of the hundreds of teams we observed used highly sophisticated electronic Web-based recording and filing systems, the seemingly simple war room of the Apple IIe project represents what we think is a clear "best practice" when it comes to capturing team memory. Beyond the notes on the walls, every core team member had his or her own three-ring notebook, complete with section headings and uniform tabs. Team leaders were responsible for the headings, and for issuing new sections when needed. Old material was discarded and replaced with the new. Even if someone on the team was not diligent in keeping his or her notebook current, everybody could count on the project leader, Mike Connor, to have a clearly organized, up-to-date notebook.

---

* Pharmaceuticals and other heavily regulated NPD efforts will need more formal documentation.

Although it may not be high tech, it was highly efficient and effective. A Web-based system may very well be able to replace that three-ring binder, but it won't replace the rich transactive memory that takes place in a good war room.

HERE AND NEAR VERSUS HITHER AND YON

Virtual Teams

Many of the teams we investigated were made up of individuals located all over the country, or the world, and in our increasingly global economy, these *virtual* teams will only increase. Naturally knowledge exchange among them is more problematic than when everybody is located in one room. The casual hallway discussions and the spontaneous luncheons are impossible, but email, videoconferencing, and the telephone make it possible to overcome many communication obstacles. The virtual team that produced the Xootr scooter provides a good example, as the three principals were located in three different parts of the country—Pennsylvania, New Hampshire, and California.

Inventor Karl Ulrich was in Philadelphia when he emailed his brother, Nathan, in Dover, New Hampshire, an outline of his concept of a kick scooter. The third member of the team was Jeff Salizar, an industrial designer in San Francisco. Through the six months of development, the three met only twice, a situation that you might expect would lead to misunderstanding and infighting. But because Nathan and Karl were brothers, they knew each other's habits and peculiarities, and how to work together. Also, Karl had worked with Salizar's firm previously on several projects, and so was willing to trust who they assigned to the project.

The communication staples between Salizar and Nathan were emails and faxes; Nathan says he has a file of about eight hundred of them that he kept in a box and referred to them when needed. During the design phase, he also kept two notebooks with drawings and the most critical faxes.

Virtual teams such as the Xootr trio are harbingers of the future. But even so, managers need to be aware that all teams, virtual or otherwise, need to have face-to-face meetings. So much of what we learn from each other depends on nonverbal cues, immediate feedback, and a certain amount of emotional content, much of which is lost by interacting at a distance. Just as the handwritten notes (perhaps with underlining for emphasis!) in the war room enhanced Apple IIe's mechanistic memory, conversation with people in the same room understandably enhances the transactive memory of everyone present. If you tell someone face-to-face why you don't agree with them, and then unequivocally state your position, you will probably both come away with a better understanding and appreciation of each other's view than by simply writing emails back and forth. In person, we are more likely to resolve the difference and come to a solution on how to proceed. Email communication during a conflict can frequently escalate rather than resolve differences.

True, telephone calls and videoconferencing can add vocal cues, but it's still not the same as a personal encounter. We're not the first to expound on the virtues of face-to-face conversation as the best way for NPD teams to communicate; earlier research by many others has explicitly demonstrated that information that is complex or ambiguous is relayed best this way. But as global teams become more prevalent, companies must learn to manage them despite their challenges. This is often best accomplished by periodically bringing the team together at critical junctures, as the Colgate Total team did, when formulating Pillars, finalizing design, reviewing market test results, and preparing for launch.

Insiders and Outsiders

Many blockbuster teams used outside contractors including designers, manufacturers, or marketers. You would think their outsider status would complicate communication, but it did not. Though not employees of the company, they operated as if they were. At Vecta, Bob Beck (the marketing director who later became the company president) and the project manager spent hours on the phone daily with the two outside designers, 5-D and IDEO, during development of the stackable Kart chair. If the outside contractors were located in another city, they might even spend an extended period of time on location at the company. At Iomega when the Zip Drive project was nearly completed, an employee from the design/marketing firm Fitch, in Columbus, Ohio, spent a month at the company's headquarters near Salt Lake City. On the Handspring Visor program, the company used outside contractors to handle the mechanical, electrical, and industrial design. All came to on-site weekly meetings with the different functional areas, scheduled back-to-back. Project marketing manager Rob Haitani says they went through every detail of the project during those sessions. "The idea was that you knew once a week we were all getting together. Jeff [Hawkins] would be there, marketing would be there," he says. " We would all make the decisions together, and everyone would have their marching orders for the week." By attending those weekly meetings, the "outsiders" were as much a part of the loop as if their offices were just down the hall.

However, we did find one major difference between the virtual teams and those where everybody is located in close proximity to one another (or *colocated,* as such teams are called): the speed with which they brought their products to market. Being located all over the country or globe extracts a heavy penalty in speed-to-market. Colocated NPD teams were more likely to meet their deadlines, while virtual teams were more likely to miss them. (See Figure 7.2.) Yet when virtual teams frequently came together face-to-face, they were better able to overcome that hurdle and more likely to meet their deadlines.

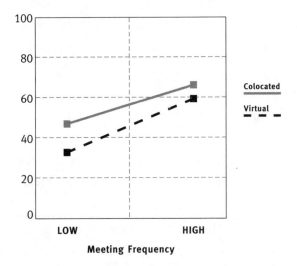

Percentage of Teams Hitting Their Deadline As a Function of Meeting Frequency

FIGURE 7.2

This figure shows the impact of meeting frequency on being able to hit the launch schedule for virtual and colocated NPD teams. We found that virtual teams were slower to market, unless they had frequent meetings. When virtual teams met less frequently, colocated teams were almost one and one-half times more likely to meet their deadlines. But when virtual teams met frequently, the advantage of colocated teams was reduced to one-tenth. Finally, most virtual teams that met frequently were able to hit their deadline, or came close.

Virtual teams can be compared to "virtual" classes where students take on-line courses from a university. Schools find that students in such courses do better when they are on campus at periodic intervals for one- to two-week programs either at the beginning or during the semester. Similarly, virtual teams should establish a pattern of regularly scheduled in-person meetings, whether they be weekly, monthly, or quarterly. That way team members can bond with their peers and managers, stay focused on the Project Pillars, be forced to meet interim goals, and keep apprised of issues that crop up.

Effective and efficient information exchange among team members cannot be ignored if you expect winning results. But good communication is one of those practices that is easy to overlook because it seems so obvious that you might assume it happens on its own. But it doesn't, as the failed teams we studied all too graphically illustrate. Different functional areas must share information early and often. Effective communication helps a dysfunctional team become functional.

Engineering and marketing, for example, even while seemingly at cross-purposes, must communicate regularly and often. By that we mean more than merely talking. Effective information exchange consists of keeping team members posted about progress toward the Project Pillars, and about challenges that emerge. Your team needs to have frequent, formal, and regular action-item-focused meetings. Your team needs to have a good system to record the team's progress, as well as a way to easily retrieve it. We call these the three Rs of information exchange: record, retrieve, review. Without effectively implementing all three, your chances of launching a blockbuster significantly decrease.

⑧ Collaboration Under Pressure

The Evolution of the Handspring Visor Team

Why do some teams never seem to pull together? Why is collaboration so hard to get sometimes? Does it happen by some sort of magic? Not at all. We found that effective teamwork is a natural by-product of implementing the other practices we've talked about and gives us the last rule of blockbuster product development: Teamwork matters. But fail to adhere to the other rules, and the team is likely not to be a "team" at all, but a bunch of bickering egos.

Effective collaboration is the result of a team sharing both a common commitment to the vision and a responsibility for getting the job done. With all the different personalities and functional areas involved in bringing a new product to market, conflicts naturally occur. The trick is to manage them so they are not detrimental to the overall effort. Conflicts over product issues actually can be beneficial to the team effort because they bring up design or manufacturing problems that others may have ignored, but that in fact need exploring and solving. Achieving this smoothly is the result of good teamwork.

Hundreds of articles and books have been written about teams and teamwork, so what can we add? NPD teams are different from many other teams—they are multifunctional and highly interdependent. The team members are experts in their respective disciplines, and not used to having to defer to someone else's judgment. Our recommendations are based on the analysis of data collected from hundreds of NPD teams, as well as in-depth case studies of blockbusters. As far as we know, our database is the only one that has empirically tested not only the components of effective teamwork in a NPD context, but also their interrelationship with the other four practices.

Teamwork was such a constant on blockbuster teams that nearly 90 percent of them rated their teams excellent in this category. (See Figure 8.1.) Without the cooperation that arises from teamwork, it is as impossible for a new product to win in the innovation race as it would be for a car to win a drag race with one cylinder misfiring. One of our most consistent findings was how necessary teamwork is for success.

THE EVOLUTION OF THE HANDSPRING VISOR TEAM

The components of teamwork and its impact can be clearly seen with the story of the Handspring Visor. How the folks who created the Palm Pilot then followed that up with the Handspring Visor demonstrates how much easier teamwork is achieved when the other practices we've talked about are in place.

The Palm Pilot, a personal digital assistant, was the fastest-selling new consumer product category in history. Introduced in early 1996, it sold faster than cell phones, pagers, even color TVs.[1] On a Palm Pilot, you could store thousands of telephone numbers and

Percentage of Teams Excelling in Teamwork

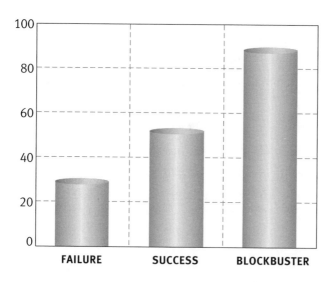

FIGURE 8.1

The blockbuster teams were three times more likely to excel in teamwork than the failed teams and more than one-third more likely than the successful ones.

birthdays, write messages, record meetings in your weekly/monthly calendar all with a handheld electronic gizmo that was so much cooler than an old datebook that always had business cards and little notes to yourself falling out of it. Furthermore, the Palm Pilot fit in your shirt pocket. It was fun to play with. Forget Filofax; PDAs were the future and the Palm Pilot was it. *PC Computing* awarded the Palm Pilot not one, but two MVP Usability Achievement Awards, one in 1996, another in 1998. In between, in 1997, it won *Newsweek*'s High Tech Gizmo of the Year Award.

But by 1998, the tight-knit group of individuals who had developed the Pilot were no longer satisfied at work. They included Jeff

Hawkins, the tall and lanky visionary who conceived the handheld computer, already a legend in the industry; Donna Dubinsky, the high-energy indispensable executive; and Ed Colligan, the quick-witted marketing genius, plus a few others. They developed the Pilot by working day and night with limited funds—after bringing out an early version that flopped. When it was time to go to market, they didn't have the millions left over to properly launch it. They needed a partner with the muscle to crack the market. U.S. Robotics, the dynamic modem maker, looked good, but instead of becoming a partner, they bought Palm Comuting outright—with its twenty-eight employees. Six months later, the Pilot 1000 and 5000 were launched.

The next year, 1997, the team woke up one morning and found that U.S. Robotics was now a part of 3Com, a global computer networking conglomerate. Colligan insisted in the business press that since their division was performing so well, 3Com wouldn't screw around with them. Soon, however, the Palm crew became restless and wanted out. They missed making their own decisions without a lot of corporate red tape. What had been an exciting venture was now simply a cog in corporate America, and the natives were becoming restless.

So in July 1998, when most people were thinking about two weeks on a beach somewhere, Hawkins and Dubinsky walked out of 3Com to form a start-up company. Hawkins—modest about his accomplishments but outspoken in his views—wanted to be his own boss again. Dubinsky says she would have followed him just about anywhere. "One of my great purposes in life has been to create an environment where Jeff Hawkins can thrive," she has said.[2] Colligan, who soon followed them, walked away from what many thought was a good shot at the presidency of the Palm division within 3Com.

Hawkins and Dubinsky settled into the downstairs of a reno-
vated Victorian house in Palo Alto with a couple of old computers
and a single potted plant while they searched for investment capital.
Hawkins went into deep-think mode, making models for the next

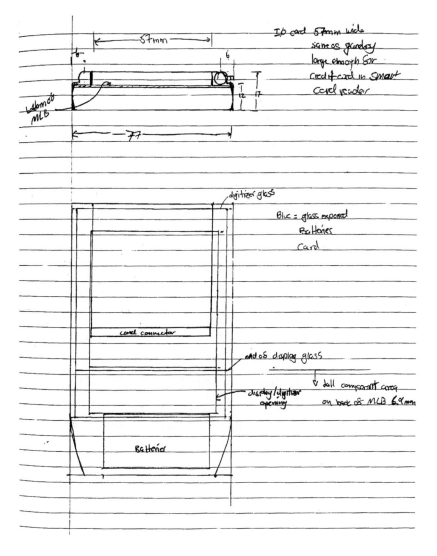

Jeff Hawkins' first sketch of the Handspring Visor. Drawing courtesy of Handspring Inc.

generation of a handheld computer in his garage, just as he had done when he created the Pilot.

By October they had moved to a third-floor office above a café on Palo Alto's funky California Avenue, lined with ethnic restaurants, where four others from the original Palm Pilot team joined them, plus an office manager who was new to the team. The Palm crew consisted of a marketing manager, two software engineers, and an electrical engineer. "All we needed to know was that it was a start-up with Jeff, Donna, and Ed," says Rob Haitani, the marketing executive who left a cushy job at 3Com. "We were basically on board before we had any discussions of compensation. This would give us a chance to work with the A Team—to get the band back together again and really focus." On their first day together, they had a "company lunch" at the dim sum place next door. The company that would be called Handspring was born.

By then, Hawkins had come up with a clear idea of what their new product would be, and came to their first meeting with a model he had whittled out of wood. He'd carried it around in his shirt pocket for weeks to see how it felt. "It" would be a handheld computer but—and it was a big but—with an expansion slot allowing users to plug-and-play modules such as games, audio players, and digital cameras, in addition to having a USB connection to synch up with your desktop computer.

The challenge was to make the device a true plug-and-play, not like the so-called plug-and-play stuff that was already out there. Not only were other devices a nightmare to install; often you would spend considerable time fiddling with it, only to discover that your computer didn't have the right graphics card or whatever to synchronize with the device, and it wouldn't work. Their Springboard, as this feature would be called, would be true

Jeff Hawkins personally whittled this first model of the Handspring Visor out of wood and carried it around in his pocket.
Photo courtesy of Handspring Inc.

plug-and-play and user friendly. It would work the way it was supposed to—easily and effortlessly.

Hawkins understood the need for rapid development. The market was dynamic with competitors in hot pursuit. He wanted the new product to be ready in twelve months, the fall of 1999. They could not afford to miss the Christmas season the following year. Cost was another target goal: the new product had to retail at $149 for the base unit, and $249 for a deluxe version. As for design, theirs was to look more upscale than the Palm Pilot. It had to be more hip. Hawkins was aiming to knock his old device down to second place.

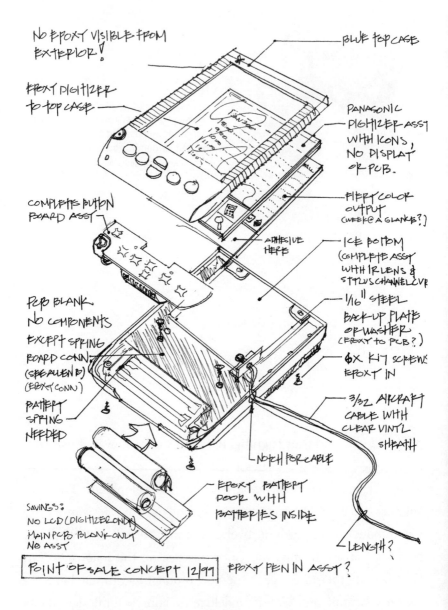

NO EPOXY VISIBLE FROM
EXTERIOR!

EPOXY DIGITIZER
TO TOP CASE

COMPLETE BUTTON
BOARD ASSY

PCB BLANK
NO COMPONENTS
EXCEPT SPRING
BOARD CONN
(SEE ALLEN E)
(EPOXY CONN)
BATTERY
SPRING
NEEDED

SAVINGS:
NO LCD (DIGITIZER ONLY)
MAIN PCB BLANK ONLY
NO ASSY

BLUE TOP CASE

PANASONIC
DIGITIZER ASSY
WITH ICONS,
NO DISPLAY
OR PCB.

FIERY COLOR
OUTPUT
(WEEK @ A GLANCE?)

ADHESIVE
HERE

ICE BOTTOM
(COMPLETE ASSY
WITH IR LENS &
STYLUS CHANNEL CVR

1/16" STEEL
BACK-UP PLATE
OR WASHER
(EPOXY TO PCB?)

6X KIT SCREWS
EPOXY IN

3/32 AIRCRAFT
CABLE WITH
CLEAR VINYL
SHEATH

NOTCH FOR CABLE

EPOXY BATTERY
DOOR WITH
BATTERIES INSIDE

LENGTH?

POINT OF SALE CONCEPT 12/99   EPOXY PEN IN ASSY?

The industrial designers' sketch of a disassembled Handspring Visor shows its components. Illustration courtesy of Handspring Inc.

Initially, the engineers were skeptical about their ability to deliver on schedule. They had a year from concept to launch, six months less than they had the first time on the original Palm Pilot. However, the team believed in Hawkins—he was why they had left their other jobs. Hawkins' conviction on this new concept bordered on messianic. The enthusiasm was contagious. "Jeff felt very strongly that he knew exactly what he wanted, that we were not going to spend any time screwing around and checking, and doing a lot of feasibility studies," says Haitani. Any misgivings were set aside as the team focused on the job at hand. The idea was that if the schedule had to be pushed back, it would be, but not now. They did not want to disappoint Hawkins.

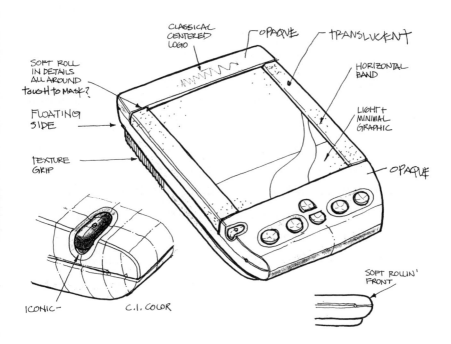

Industrial designers' illustration of the Handspring Visor fully assembled. Courtesy of Handspring Inc.

Their office was primitive: computers were whatever they brought in from home; a cheesy old dot matrix printer stood in for a copier; personal accounts were used for email. They joked about their lack of corporate creature comforts those first few weeks, but Haitani says their sense of mission and commitment to the team more than made up for things missing. "Everyone had confidence that the others on the team were going to deliver for you," he recalls. "There was zero frustration, zero distraction, and everyone was pulling their weight." That kind of faith in each other instilled the conviction that they could pull this off. "You know that you are working with superstar material," Haitani reflects. "It was just a heavenly experience."

As a team, they had several things going for them: they had worked together before and so knew each other's strengths; they trusted each other's abilities; their cramped quarters and the local restaurant row where they frequently ate together facilitated communication. They stopped each other in the hall, they walked over to each other's cubicle, they met at lunch. Information flowed as easily as water over a fall. "Donna used to say we were kind of like the old married couple who finishes each other's sentences," Haitani observes. "We knew each other's habits." So plugged in were they that the only review meetings they had were ones with the outside mechanical engineering team they hired. For their internal status updates, Haitani would drop by everyone's cubicle once a week for five minutes and write up a report.

Right on schedule, the Handspring Visor with the Springboard plug-and-play was ready to go the following fall. They announced their new product with a national advertising and PR campaign in technology and business magazines, and at first it was only available through the Internet. They thought Internet-only distribution would give them a chance to ramp up their manufacturing capabilities while demand built slowly. Ha! The response was overwhelming, to say the least. In the first month, the Visor captured a quarter of the U.S. PDA sales in the United States, an unheard-of volume for a new product competing in an established market. But by working long hours together, they got through the crunch. Everybody pitched in and took their turn in a "war room," where they tracked down back orders, or dealt with angry customers waiting for their Visor. If you were really fuming, you might actually get Hawkins or Dubinsky on the phone. After some tense weeks of manually filling orders, and reworking the Web site to be able to handle the volume, the operation smoothed out.

Within months the company went public with a $200 million initial public offering, and both Hawkins and Dubinsky found themselves on the Forbes list of "400 richest people in America." A little more than a year later, Handspring introduced a remarkable innovation, the VisorPhone, which allowed you to turn your handheld into a cell phone! That day the company's stock galloped up to $81 per

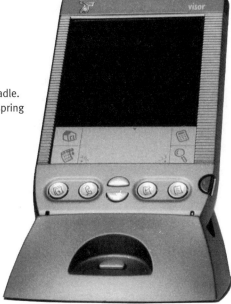

The Handspring Visor Prism in its cradle. This product helped establish Handspring as a leading PDA manufacturer.
Photograph by Daria Amato.

share, a gain of 119 percent from the initial offering. With over 25.3 million Visors sold worldwide, it became the second largest provider of PDAs. Sales for 2001 reached $123.8 million.

HOW TO MAKE A TEAM WORK

You might be saying to yourself, well, that's a good story, but it's unique. Handspring was a small start-up with people who had worked together before. What about my company—how can you inspire that kind of collaboration among a group of people brought together from different functions, all squabbling over who's going to do what and when? You may not have a genius like Jeff Hawkins, or a consummate executive like Donna Dubinsky, you're thinking. True, the collaborative spirit on the Handspring Visor team may seem unusual, but we believe it is possible to duplicate and we saw it on the vast majority of the blockbuster teams.

Teamwork Is a Result of Implementing the Other Practices. How did blockbuster teams achieve effective teamwork? We found that teamwork was not a result of people liking one another. What we observed is that they worked as a unit because they had strong participation from senior management; had a unified goal (Project Pillars); effectively shared information; and each had clearly delineated roles and responsibilities. Engineers knew what their jobs were, as did people in marketing, manufacturing, and so on. By implementing the other practices, effective teamwork emerged. When we looked closely at our data, using *multiple regression* analysis,* we

---

* Multiple regression is a statistical technique that determines whether multiple variables can predict another variable. It allowed us to determine which variables made a statistically significant contribution to the variable teamwork that we are trying to predict.

found that excellence in the other four practices could actually predict the level of teamwork with a relatively high degree of accuracy,
and each practice added something unique. (See Figure 8.2.) As a
team's support of the vision and Project Pillars increased, so did teamwork; when we factored in having a hard deadline (Lickety Stick rule
number three!), teamwork improved even more; when the quality of

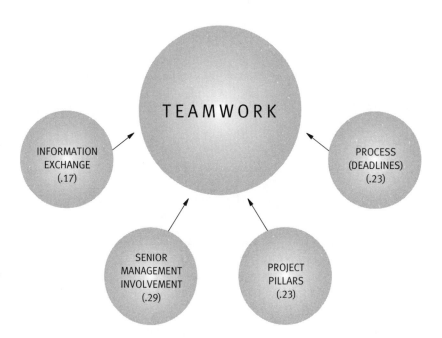

Regression Analysis of
Four Critical Practices and Teamwork

FIGURE 8.2

This figure depicts the results of a multiple regression analysis that examined the
simultaneous impact of the four other critical practices (senior management
involvement, Project Pillars, Lickety Stick process, information exchange) on teamwork. Here we show the contribution of each of the practices (coefficients) that
impact teamwork. All of the practices are statistically significant, indicating that they
each make an important and independent contribution to teamwork effectiveness.[3]

knowledge exchange was high, so was teamwork; when senior management was enthusiastically involved, teamwork soared.

What was so surprising about effective collaboration was how easily it was achieved when the other practices were implemented. The more practices a team excelled at, the greater the likelihood of achieving the esprit de corps that is so necessary if the project is to succeed big. (See Figure 8.3.)

Percentage of Teams Excelling in Teamwork When Other Practices Are Done Well

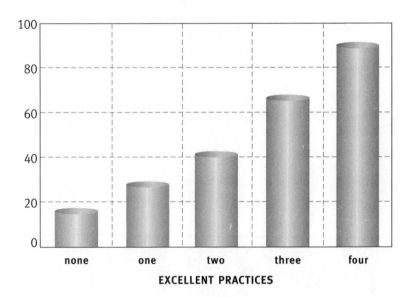

EXCELLENT PRACTICES

FIGURE 8.3

To demonstrate the relationship between the other practices and teamwork, we subdivided our entire sample into five groups. Those that excelled in all four practices, those that excelled in three, two, one, and none. We then looked at the percentage of teams in each group that excelled in teamwork. What we found was a dramatic increase in the level of teamwork as the number of practices implemented increased. For example, if four of the other practices were implemented, the team was almost six times more likely to excel in teamwork than a team that excelled in none of the practices.

You might still be thinking that the Handspring Visor team is a special case because of the people involved. Perhaps your company doesn't have a brainy visionary that everybody wants to work with. However, if you analyze how the Handspring team worked together, you will see that they had incorporated all of the other practices we're talking about: (1) senior management support; (2) clear and stable vision with Project Pillars; (3) excellent information exchange; and (4) an improvisation process that included an aggressive deadline with rapid successive prototyping. On this final point, the Handspring team had the benefit of the earlier products they had developed—the failed PDA (Zoomer, released before the Palm Pilot) and the Palm Pilot itself—essentially became their market trials for what became the Visor. Additionally, once Hawkins had a working model of the Visor, he took it wherever he went, say, his dentist's office, and would pull it out and start using it. People naturally asked about it, and their reactions confirmed he was onto something. And the team had a hard deadline: the gift-giving season of 1999. Someone else would beat them if they didn't hurry.

It was only one year away.

DEADLINES AND DINOSAURS

One unexpected finding of our research was the significance of a hard deadline on teamwork. That a deadline would help coalesce the team didn't initially surface in our quantitative data, but it immediately did in our interviews. The positive effect of a hard deadline on teamwork was a consistent finding on all blockbuster teams. But how can a hard deadline—which seems to have nothing to do with teamwork—have such a profound impact on team behavior? In a nutshell, a deadline galvanizes a team to get the job done, and pushes all other considerations—such as petty interpersonal conflicts—aside.

Conventional wisdom says teams methodically go through four stages: In the *forming* stage, members get to know one another, and begin to establish a framework for working together. In the *storming* stage, members disagree about how to proceed. In the *norming* stage, they develop camaraderie and begin to work together. Finally, in the *performing* stage, they get the job done.

This four-part sequence was determined by observing psychotherapy groups, where the focus of the research was the psychosocial and emotional component of team behavior, which includes interpersonal dependency, control, and intimacy. However, when we began to examine blockbuster NPD teams with real deadlines, we found that they cooperated quite differently. This was especially true of teams like the Handspring team where the members had worked together closely before.

Teams made up of people who know one another well approach their new task with a backlog of knowledge about how they work together, and so are able to jump right in with complementary behaviors that will reach their goal quickly. Many of our blockbuster teams, just like the Handspring squad, consisted of people who had worked together previously.

Obviously it's not possible to have every NPD consist of people who have been together before on a project—there's always a first time. And that's where a hard deadline helps. To understand how, consider the dynamics of most teams—people from different functions who may not know each other come together to work for a common goal. They get started on the project, but everything moves slowly for a while. How long depends on the length of the project. One study of eight real work teams discovered that although teams vary considerably in the way they initially approach their task, every team stays with their original behavior—usually less than efficient—until they have used up approximately half the time allotted.[4] At the midpoint, groups alter their behavior, quickly finding the wherewithal to drop old, ineffective behaviors, seek additional support from outsiders if necessary, and develop new modes of working. Once this transition is over, teams make dramatic progress because they've got a deadline to meet! The really successful teams adopted this pattern, no matter how long they had to complete their project. This shift in the team's behavior is called *punctuated equilibrium,*[5] a phrase borrowed from evolutionary biology. Take away the deadline, or have a deadline that is vague or too far away, and teams will continue their pokey behavior, and not adapt to finish the project on time.

They are like the dinosaurs who became extinct because they couldn't adapt. A controversial theory holds that long intervals of evolutionary equilibrium, in which changes are slight, are punctuated with short, revolutionary transitions when species became extinct and are replaced by new forms of life. Think of the typical team as one whose equilibrium is shattered by the imposition of a deadline, followed with a burst of adaptation during which they come up with new ways to get the job done on time. The dinosaurs couldn't adapt; neither did the teams who failed.

Deadlines Dissolve Disagreement. A deadline serving as an incentive for teams to pull together works only if the team has clear and stable Project Pillars. Any ambiguity on the vision can lead to chaos.

Any differences of opinion that do exist should be quickly resolved or quashed. Listen to Bob Beck, the mastermind behind the Kart chairs: "There was friction, but somehow they [the team members] got over it. I was willing to say, 'This is what we're doing. That's final. Over with.' Most of all we didn't have a lot of time to deal with the friction."

We heard the same from other teams: a deadline forced everyone to overcome their interpersonal problems quickly, or simply table them. If you don't have time to massage your grievance, it's likely to blow over. The vast majority of blockbuster teams had no training in conflict management, listening and collaborative communication, all considered hallmarks of "teamwork" training, but because the groundwork was in place—the four other critical practices—conflicts were kept to a minimum. Trainers who specialize in listening and communication were not needed. "Team chemistry" was not a concept that blockbuster teams seemed to bother about. A famous illustration of this is the Oakland A's baseball team of the 1970s.

> United only by their dislike of Finley [the owner], they battled one another with their fists in the locker room. But for five years in a row they were also the best team in their division in the American League and three times in a row—1972, 1973, 1974—they proved themselves to be the best in baseball—the first club other than the Yankees ever to take three consecutive World Championships.[6]

Even though they did not like each other, they were committed to winning and so put their differences aside on the field.

THE MYTH OF POSITIVE TEAM CHEMISTRY

Similarly, we found that on teams developing new products that take a large leap forward—versus a small incremental change—such as the SoundStation and the Zip Drive, intellectual argument was actually a plus. Here, the team maverick is not afraid to bring up problems with the design, and who is willing to argue them moves the creative process forward not backward in the search for ingenious solutions. The yes-men who "go along to get along" are not the original thinkers and problem-solvers a blockbuster team needs.

Consequently, many of our blockbusters did not score high on "team chemistry." On the Motorola team that developed the hugely successful StarTAC cell phone, for instance, "there was not a lot of teamwork going on—it was more or less a competitive atmosphere," says Albert Nagele, who designed the original model. On the Polycom SoundStation, Jeff Rodman recalls that the software people were "off in the stratosphere" at the same time the mechanical design guys were in Asia looking for vendors. Individual team members did most of their work independently, and only saw each other when they needed to. "Once you got the information you wanted, you drove back to your office." This doesn't sound like much "chemistry" to us.

What you need on the team are your best original thinkers, people not afraid to speak their mind, but not the naysayers either, who find fault with everything yet offer no constructive suggestions on how to improve anything. Their negative attitude is destructive to any project and demoralizing to any team. Unless they change their attitude, show them the door—the way Kim Edwards did at Iomega.

On the blockbuster teams, conviviality may not have been the norm, but on the failed teams there was outright dissension. A shared vision and strong senior management involvement kept everybody in line on the blockbuster teams. Even if someone didn't like the guy at the next bench, they were working toward the same goal, and interpersonal conflicts were not allowed to overtake the team *gestalt*. The dissension on the failed teams occurred because team members did not have clear Project Pillars nor did they agree to them; also, senior management did not pay enough attention to the team or step in to settle arguments.

For example, Barry Yarkoni, the head of marketing on the failed Apple III, admits that he thought the engineers "were screwing up the product right from the beginning, and I was trying to get it steered back in the right direction. . . . It was not a cooperative relationship. There were hostilities." The Lisa project was the same story. It was a constant annoyance to the engineers that marketing was in control of the project. "Marketing never appreciated the amount of work required to build all of the technology, so there was always this tension that was really over the schedule," comments Wayne Rosing, who was running pretty much all of engineering on the project. "I don't think that because you've got an MBA from Harvard you have an intrinsic ability to design products in the computer business, which was what a lot of these people thought." With so much friction, no wonder there was no real teamwork and the result: failure.

SECURING BUY-IN OF THE VISION

The failure of the Lisa project probably would not even have happened if the team had bought into a shared vision of the project. (See Figure 8.4.) For a team to be successful, first, there needs to be clear Pillars and then all need to enthusiastically support them.

Percentage of Teams That Supported the Vision

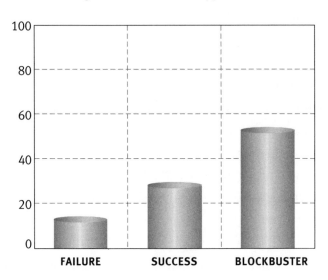

FIGURE 8.4

Blockbuster teams were four times more likely than failed teams to completely support the vision for the new product, and almost twice as likely as successful teams.

Without that buy-in, it is like musicians in an orchestra playing off different sheets of music. The result is chaos.

How do you secure buy-in? Sometimes everyone supports the project because it is such a hot idea and they want to be a part of the action. Here you get "design by enthusiasm" as Andy Hertzfeld, one of the early Apple employees, describes it.

Or maybe the idea of working with a certain team leader—someone everyone looks up to—galvanizes everybody. Consider what happened at Handspring. The team consisted of people who left their jobs to work with Hawkins. If a star like Hawkins, or your star performers, are involved, the general belief will be that the project must be a good one. Top people attract other top people.

Hawkins himself has all the qualities of an inspiring leader. Not only is he renowned in the industry, but people call him modest and relaxed. He likes to joke around. He doesn't seem like a salesman, but he is messianic when it comes to his ideas. Sometimes you need his kind of "salesmanship" to win over a team's full and complete support.

Though salesmanship is ignored in mainstream project management training, we found that often the best project managers turn out to be good salesmen for the project, because, in effect, they're selling the vision of the product to the team members—as well as to people at their level in other departments, and possibly, even to senior management to get their buy-in, involvement, and full support. A great many of the project leaders on the blockbuster teams had characteristics similar to charismatic or transformational leaders— they were terrific salespeople, in other words. They were leaders whose personal charisma inspired, excited, and motivated the team to greatness.

One final technique for securing buy-in is to provide the parameters but let the team figure out the specifics of implementation. The Project Pillars that IBM's CEO gave to its PC team left plenty of room for creativity and initiative—*beat Apple and do it in one year.* "It was a very busy and creative two weeks," recalls Bill Lowe, the initial project leader. "It was very exciting."

The opposite of exciting is what you get when a vision is ambiguous and constantly changing. Earlier we discussed how vision instability led to marketplace flubs such as the white elephants called the DataMaster and the PC jr. over at IBM, and the Lisa computer and the Apple III at Apple Computer. "We had a major war going on," says Barry Yarkoni of the III. "Engineering basically wanted a souped-up Apple II, while marketing was adamant that the cash cow, the II, was not to be cannibalized." A similar situation happened on Lisa, says Lisa marketing manager, Barry Smith. "There wasn't an agreed upon demarcation between marketing and engineering." Somebody with authority needed to step in and call an end to the turf battles, and unfortunately at Apple and IBM for those projects, no one did.

FOR A-1 RESULTS, PICK "THE A TEAM"

Teamwork or not, dissension or not, blockbuster teams are not made up of mediocre people. Yes, this is self-evident, but by this we mean more than just assuring that your top brains are assigned to the new project. The confidence they can instill in the team is infectious. If senior management believes in the team's ability to succeed, and succeed in a big way, the prophecy is likely to be self-fulfilling.[7] Everyone fortunate enough to be tapped for the team will believe in the team's absolute ability to win. Your team will likely create a blockbuster because they believe they can.

Furthermore, if you have followed the first golden practice for blockbuster innovation—have a high-level manager on the team as an active participant—you have implicitly informed the team that its work is important. Think of Kim Edwards talking to the engineers every morning. Think of Brian Hinman traveling around the country with prototypes. Think of Jeff Hawkins designing the product himself. When a senior manager is intimately involved with the team, he or she gives the team a kind of golden glow. The team has "bureaucratic immunity"[8] from a possibly stodgy corporate culture that might inhibit them, and the authority to move forward with creative solutions.

TEAM SIZE

How big is the optimum team size? We would like to say that size doesn't matter, but reality is more complicated. Team size is dictated by the complexity and nature of the new product and although the literature stresses that the best size for an effective team is ten or fewer,[9] our blockbuster teams ranged from three to twenty, and even larger—up to two thousand (a NASA project). Their average size was eighteen. But team size numbers are somewhat misleading because as the launch date neared, the teams ramped up and many grew to over a hundred people. While size did not statistically impact success of the teams that we studied, we found that failed teams tended to be larger—with an average size of forty-nine.

Deciding exactly who was on the core team and who was not is not a fine science. When do you start counting? Do you start when the idea was conceived? When the first prototype was made? When the product was released to manufacturing? Launched? Others have suggested[10] that one way to determine who is on the core team is to consider who would be asked to go on a trip to, say, the Bahamas, for a week as a thank-you for a wildly successful job. Those who would have a seat on the plane comprise the core team.

A CHECKLIST FOR COLLABORATION

So, what is the short list of things to do if you want to create teams that collaborate? First, give the team some real power by having the power on the team—a high-level manager who plays an active, participatory role. Second, establish a clear vision. Third, get team members to enthusiastically buy into that vision. Fourth, set a hard deadline, such as a national trade show, a date laid down by the CEO, or a large customer meeting where you will showcase the product to potential customers. Fifth, put your best people on the team. If you do these things, your team members will have a greater probability of working effectively together.

We've now given you the five blockbuster practices for new product development, and demonstrated how they complement each other synergistically. One or two won't do the trick. The vast majority (74 percent) of the blockbusters implemented all five practices. And while we can't guarantee your resulting product will be a blockbuster, we can say that it will most likely come close if you do them all and do them well. If you do, you and your team will have an intense but exhilarating time during the process. You have nothing to lose but success itself.

Throughout the book, we have dealt with products that represent evolutionary advances over what was currently available; in the next chapter, on radical innovation, we deal with discoveries that herald entirely new market categories with unproven technologies.

9

What About Radical Innovation?

Seeing the Light—
Corning's Fiber Breakthrough

Products that are unlike anything seen before present the biggest challenge and the biggest opportunity. The products we've talked about so far represent innovations that primarily were improvements on what was currently available. Black and Decker's Dustbuster was a new kind of product, a handheld vacuum, but it is nonetheless a vacuum cleaner. The Gillette Sensor razor gave a smoother shave, but it is still basically a razor. Marvin's Double-Hung windows were unquestionably better-looking than competing products, but they are windows, and everyone knows what a window is. The market for them could be tested because the companies making them were sailing into already charted waters.

But there is another type of product, a *radical* innovation that uses untested technology and creates a new market category. The first television is one such product; Intel's smart card—a credit card–sized device that can hold mountains of data and may revolutionize how information is stored—is another; and DuPont's Kevlar, the material that goes into bulletproof vests, is a third. Such ground-breaking products present several challenges.

Not only is the technology undiscovered and unproven, so is its market. You can't accurately concept test a radically new idea or sketch that is so unlike anything available because no one knows what it will ultimately be like when it is actually produced and offered for sale.

The road to finding the right solutions to these problems is long, and the route to market success circuitous. But when we looked at how companies developed radical innovations that became block-busters, we discovered that they indeed had applied the five key practices, only in a somewhat different way from how they are implemented for evolutionary innovations. Senior management support is likely to consist of funding, not day-to-day involvement; the vision and Project Pillars may not emerge for several years; concept testing in the early stages is impossible because the product is so far from being market ready, and the market itself is questionable; information is best exchanged only among team members, and not with people from other teams. The meandering story of Corning's development of optical fiber that ultimately transformed both the company and long-distance communications demonstrates how radical innovations are created and brought to market.

CORNING'S FIBER BREAKTHROUGH

When Corning began developing optical fibers in the 1950s, little was certain about them. Though it was known that glass could carry light pulses, measured in decibels, just what could be efficiently achieved was unknown.

What are optical fibers? They are hair-thin strands of glass through which light is channeled by a property known as *total internal reflection*. The mathematics behind the concept were worked out as far back as 1820 by Frenchman Augustine-Jean Fresnel, but ninety years would pass before his equations would be extended to glass wires. Over the next half century, slow-but-sure advances around the world led to optical fibers that could carry light over short distances—but the light lost 99 percent of its strength in as short a distance as thirty feet. Aptly named, these *high-loss* fibers were in use by the 1960s in night-vision devices in army tanks, in automobile dashboards, and in instruments that allowed doctors to scan the inside of a human body and engineers to look inside industrial equipment.

Corning, at the time, was one of the main suppliers of the high-loss optical fibers, though the program was not expected to yield appreciable profits. However, Corning continued to develop and manufacture them due to the company's involvement in glass and ceramics-based businesses, and its contracts to supply high-loss fibers to the U.S. military.

Then in 1966 two English scientists, Charles Kao and George Hockham, published a widely circulated paper in which they theorized that the main reason for the high losses of light in optical fibers was not the glass itself, but other chemicals besides silica found in glass. They postulated that removing these impurities should reduce the light loss significantly—from the current thousand decibels per kilometer to less than twenty decibels per kilometer (20 dB/km), a level where at least 1 percent of the light entering a fiber would emerge after traveling a distance of one kilometer. Kao and Hockham further hypothesized that when such a low-loss fiber was produced, amplifiers could boost the light signal along the transmission path, much the same way that repeaters amplified weak signals along conventional telephone lines. The landmark paper set the goal of 20 dB/km for researchers around the world. Once that level of light loss was possible, optical fiber would be feasible for use in long-distance telecommunication.

Before the year was out, Corning was looking into ways to develop low-loss fibers. The CEO at the time, Amory Houghton, remembers Allan Dawson, the head of the television division, saying, "I don't know where it's going, but we need to be behind it." Although Corning executives talked to several potential lead-user customers for the as-yet-undiscovered breakthrough, exactly what or who or how big the market was for fibers was unclear. "We knew it was big and that it was telephone," says Bill Armistead, then Corning's R&D director. That was about all they knew. Charles Lucy, who became the business leader of the project, recalls the uncertainty they all felt:

> Nobody knew what had to be done, so there was no way to know how much it was going to cost. Nobody knew what you could do, so there was no way to figure a payoff. The application was for picture phones. At some of the world's fairs, they were talking about picture phones in your home. . . . Then people were talking about conference centers, when business people could come into a conference center and there would be picture phones available, and you could run picture-phone conferences. Where optical fibers would end up was pure speculation.

With so many unknowns and formidable technical obstacles ahead, Corning, though a technology-driven company, was reluctant to make a big investment in the fiber-optics project. In the lab, only physicist Robert Maurer had been working on it, and only in his spare time. Maurer described his job as "being able to make something that you could hold up and show someone, say in development or marketing," and tell them to find an application for it. But after the Kao and Hockham paper, a worldwide race was on to reach 20 dB/km. Scientists at the British Post Office, operators of the British phone system, specifically stated they were looking into optical fiber to make the picture phone a reality. In the United States, Bell Labs, AT&T's research and development arm, was Corning's main competition.

Two newly minted Ph.D.s, Donald Keck and Peter Schultz, joined Maurer at Corning in 1967. They had one big advantage: they did not know that the goal of 20 dB/km was impossible. After three years of frustrating experiments that seemingly went down a black hole, late one August afternoon in 1970, Keck made a new mix of silica and drew it out into fibers. He decided to take a quick measurement. As Ira Magaziner and Mark Patinkin relate in their book *The Silent War:*

He [Keck] put the fiber on the rig. He bent over his microscope and began to line up the laser. He watched as the pinpoint beam got closer and closer to the core. Suddenly, he got hit with a bright beam of light, right in the pupil. "Good grief," he said, "What do I have here?" It must have been a mistake. The laser was badly aligned perhaps, reflecting off something else. But he looked again, and it was the same bright beam. And yes, the laser was perfectly aligned, in the heart of the core. He looked at the fiber's other end—it showed a brighter spot of the light than he'd yet seen. Finally, he realized what had happened. They'd done it. And they'd done it so well, the laser had burst down the core, bounced off the other end, and reflected back. He looked to check the decibel level, the light loss—

attenuation, in the language of the lab. Would it be under the magic twenty? He couldn't imagine it possible. But it was. Donald Keck's gauge told him light loss was under twenty. By now it was 5:30. He rushed out of the lab. Maurer was gone, so he went to two or three other offices—no one. Then the elevator doors opened. It was Bill Armistead, Corning's head of research. "Hey," said Keck, "you want to see something neat?" The two went into the lab and shared the moment. Keck would say later that he could just about feel the spirit of Edison. Usually lab notebooks are fairly dry. On that day in 1970, Keck's entry is there for posterity. "Attenuation equals 16 db," it says.[1]

He followed that with a single word: "Whoopie!"

Excitement over the breakthrough ran high—maybe the picture phone in every home was possible! But roadblocks would derail the use of optical fibers for years. Not only was the technology to harness the discovery a long way off; there was another obstacle, and it was a big one. AT&T had recently upgraded their manufacturing capabilities to make copper cable, the medium for their telephone lines. "They had an installed base of copper cable that was out of this world," remarks Tom MacAvoy, who was COO of Corning's glass works division. Since AT&T's rates were based on long-term amortization—thirty to forty years, "the last thing in the world they wanted to do was to write this off," he adds.

At the time, AT&T basically had a hammerlock on telecommunications in this country, controlling 85 percent of the market. Without a financial incentive, the company simply wasn't interested in optical fiber. Even the researchers at Bell Labs put their work on the back burner. So did the British Post Office, saying the picture phone was an invention for the next century. Other phone and cabling companies reacted similarly—optical fibers were untested,

Laser light traveling through coils of Corning's optical fibers reenacting the initial discovery. Photo courtesy of Corning Incorporated, Corning, N.Y.

expensive, not worth the risk. The prospect of reaping any commercial benefit appeared to be lost. There was no way to establish anything resembling Project Pillars, or determine what the commercial application might be. "The increased market uncertainty was more significant than the technological achievement," recalls Lucy. "We were all dressed up and had nowhere to go."

Corning's investment up until then had been primarily in research, with a modest budget—less than a million dollars—compared to what opening a plant would cost. Though the company was filling small orders from the military for optical fibers, Corning's financial

people saw that any chance of success demanded a huge commitment, one they did not want to make with such questionable
prospects. "It was a big deep hole and people were saying, Why keep
putting money in it?" explains David Duke, who would later become
head of the program.

But Lucy was determined not to let the optical-fiber program
die. He and Maurer calculated that if they could improve engineering efficiencies, optical fibers could effectively compete with inexpensive copper wire that was selling for cents per meter. He looked
to outside partners to share the risk. No one in America was interested. Ultimately Lucy was able to spark interest from abroad, and
brought in five companies and two governmental agencies to invest
approximately $100,000 annually for five years, in exchange for a
licensing option in their country when the product was ready.[2] Their
investment would pay off, but it would take a while.

In 1973, Lucy remembers writing a "business plan"—he doesn't
call it that—around the estimated cost of opening a pilot plant, an
investment of about one million dollars: "First, you calculated what
you needed to justify the pilot plant, and that's the number we used.
Nobody could know the 'correct' number. It was a shell game. Who
knew what the market would be? Nobody even knew if we could
make the optical cables in commercial quantities."

His creative accounting was convincing. Senior management
gave him the go-ahead, and the following year a pilot plant was up
and running. Corning began selling optical fiber cables to its partners and a few other companies that wanted to evaluate them.[3]
Although the end use of optical fiber was not yet clearly in sight, senior management believed in it. James Fisk, the retired and normally
reticent president of Bell Labs, had joined Corning's board. "Fisk
didn't say a lot in meetings, but when we got into this optical fiber

business, he pulled a cigar out of his mouth and said, 'This one is really important,' " says MacAvoy. "And he stuck the cigar back in his mouth."[4] CEO Houghton, who was on the boards of New York Telephone and IBM, began to see the possibilities. The joint development partners were still paying their share of the tab, and they could not be ignored. A final factor was what Houghton called "the fear factor." Some of Corning's other businesses were bleeding money, and thousands of people had been laid off. "In 1975 we went from 45,000 people to 29,000 people in four months," he recalls. The company needed a new profit center. Maybe optic fiber would be it.

Once Houghton became embroiled in a project, the company was sure to follow. "Every so often you bet your company on something," Houghton explains. R&D director William Armistead says once Houghton became convinced that optical fibers had legs he was tenacious: "He made us all pitch in and pursue it. There was not much argument about it—he would not stand for any argument. He said, 'Do it!' If you talked to people in the company, they would say, 'Oh, we're spending so much money on this thing, and what will it ever amount to . . . ' but Amo had a hold of it, you see, and there was no stopping the CEO!"[5]

TIME TO COMMERCIALIZE—AT LAST

In 1976, things began—barely—to coalesce. ITT's British subsidiary installed an optical-fiber system in a local police department, connecting a video display with the central processing unit of their computer. The information was only carried over several hundred yards at the rate of ten megabits per second, but it was an important milestone—it was the world's first commercial use of optical fiber. Later that year there were two significant applications of optical fibers: a British cable television company laid an optical fiber telecommunications trunk line, and in the United States, TelePrompter Manhattan Cable Television Corporation, then the largest cable company in the world, installed an 800-foot system that transmitted signals to receiving equipment thirty-four floors below; the television signals were then sent over traditional cables to subscribers.

These efforts helped give Corning the confidence to continue. Corning plunged ahead, and transformed the project from one that was pursued in the cracks to a full-fledged venture. David Duke, a veteran Corning manager, was put in charge of commercializing fiber optics. Yet the final end use of the product was still unknown. A consulting firm wrote up a report the size of a small-city phone book stating that the potential lay in local area networks (LANs) for computers, primarily because IBM and Hewlett-Packard were talking about it. But many at Corning didn't believe it, including Duke. "We knew our business well, and we felt computer LANs would not happen for ten years, and that the opportunity was telephone companies and cable vision, not military, and not computer links," he recalls.

A decade had gone by and millions had been spent, but a formal marketing analysis—or even a back-of-the-napkin analysis—still was virtually impossible. Lucy says that if any "by-the-book marketing guy" had been involved, "it never would have gotten off the ground." Not only was there no marketing plan, and no profit-and-loss statement, the people running the program could not be certain it would ever succeed. "The program was not driven by traditional market evaluation or criteria," he observes. "Vision drove it. Technological enthusiasm drove it." Even for a company that is research-driven, it was a lot to ask.

That is not to say that management didn't try to figure out what possible use could be made of optical fibers. Duke recalls that when he had to give presentations to key company executives, he would be asked, "What will the returns be?" and the financial people would want to see the cash flows, he says. "Depending on what scenario we chose, we would get sales volumes plus or minus three factories."

Yet there were clues that fiber optics would be the breakthrough Corning was banking on. GTE installed a test optical fiber network that carried phone calls more than five miles. The Defense Department looked to Corning to develop new optical-fiber systems, and the U.S. Army announced that it would replace its copper wire with optical fiber in its tactical communications systems.[6]

Though these contracts and possibilities were encouraging, the overall practical application for widespread telecommunication use was still elusive. Without any great interest from AT&T or their overseas partners, Corning's senior management again switched their target back to interoffice applications. The vision for the product had changed from picture phones, to long-distance telecommunications, to local area networks. It was as if senior management was in a fun house with doors opening up and slamming shut and opening up again as they made their way through.

Nonetheless, CEO Houghton felt it was better to risk being saddled with an idle plant than to lose the lead the company had built up, so in 1979, Corning opened a 38,000-square-foot manufacturing facility for its optical fiber production in Wilmington, North Carolina. Shortly thereafter, a breakthrough in the technology allowed Corning to reach new distance records for transmission. You would think by now Corning would get a break—but AT&T still had their outlay in expensive copper wire and showed no interest. Sales had only reached some $10 million, while the investment was approaching $100 million. And Corning had yet to win a single major order.

But outside circumstances would change the landscape dramatically, and at last Corning would have the right product at the right time. In 1982, the U.S. government split up AT&T, giving outside companies the right to compete against the established behemoth. They would look for a competitive advantage, and find it in fiber optics, which can carry 65,000 times more information than conventional copper wire. MCI was interested.

Up to this time, Corning had made only small quantities of the type of (single-mode) fiber MCI wanted to buy. Allan Dawson, the U.S. head of Corning's German partner, Siecor, recalled the meeting with MCI:

> We had never made more than three inches of single-mode fiber at that point* . . . MCI told us what we had to sell it for. David [Duke] guessed the cost from a fiber standpoint, and I guessed from a cable standpoint. We were basing the figure all on our prior experience with multimode fiber. David and I were handing little pieces of paper back and forth during the meeting. I wrote on one piece of paper, "Dave, do you think we can do it?" And on another I wrote, "What about the cabling and all the other stuff?" His reply: "Yes." We then took a contract for $90 million for the delivery of the single-mode fiber cable to MCI, which was the first real piece of business we ever booked.

---

* This was obviously an exaggeration said for effect, since to make a fiber of the kind he was talking about, you need to make at least a kilometer, probably more.

Other telecommunications companies followed suit, as did AT&T, now aware they would be left behind with outdated technology if they didn't get into fiber optics. Nearly overnight, demand outstripped supply. Corning's position reversed from having excess capacity to not having enough. In 1982, MCI's order of 150,000 kilometers of fibers alone exceeded the total capacity of the plant, and Corning did not even yet know definitively if they could produce single-mode fiber at the prices customers wanted to buy it, and still make a profit. Duke then took a gutsy move. He sought the largest expenditure in Corning's history ($100 million) to boost Wilmington's capacity.

THE INVESTMENT PAYS OFF

By the end of 1983, Corning's long investment in fiber optics began to pay off, and pay off handsomely. The market exploded in all directions: AT&T had installed nearly 200,000 miles of optic fiber, the local area networks for computers fell into place, and fiber was becoming commercially competitive with satellite communications opening up transoceanic cabling as a market. Even home-based systems were gaining interest. As a test, the state-owned French telephone company connected fifteen hundred homes in the Biarritz area in an optical fiber network to provide customers with videophone service, videotext, and cable television. In the United States, Times Fiber was installing a network to distribute cable-television programming in several apartment and condominium complexes. In 1983 alone, the total United States optical fiber market was estimated to be over 339,000 kilometers worth nearly $121.8 million.

Four years later, in 1987, Corning's annual optical fiber sales surpassed $200 million and reportedly contributed $75 million to the company's operating income. More than 15 million kilometers of long-distance optical fibers have been sold worldwide, and the forecast is for sales to reach $1.2 trillion by 2007.

Corning's optic fiber has been singled out numerous times for its technical achievement and commercial value. Among its laurels are the *Photonics Spectra* 1999 Circle of Excellence Award; the *Laser Focus World*'s Commercial Technology Achievement Award, the *Fiberoptic Product News* Annual Technology Award, *R&D* magazine's R&D 100 Award for 1999 and 2001. In 1995, Corning optical fiber was awarded the Malcolm Baldrige National Quality Award—Corning is the only optical fiber manufacturer to receive this prestigious honor.

Corning's perseverance with the development of optical fibers, pouring money year after year down what Duke called "a big deep

Thin hairlike strands of optical glass fiber show light that carries today's telecommunications. Corning's optical fibers established a multibillion-dollar business for the company. Photo courtesy of Corning Incorporated, Corning, N.Y.

hole," transformed the company from a glass manufacturer to a leader in telecommunications and revolutionized long-distance communication in the process.

When we analyzed how the company developed—and succeeded—with the radical innovation of optical fiber, we saw that they had indeed implemented the five critical practices of developing a blockbuster. But they did it somewhat differently from what we observed for incremental innovations. We'll look at each of the five practices in the context of creating a radically new blockbuster product.

SENIOR MANAGEMENT SUPPORT

No doubt about it, senior management plays a critical role in all new products. Without their full support any project is likely to fail, and this is especially true in radical innovation because these types of projects typically require extraordinarily long lead time—years—to develop, and senior management must fund the project while it may seem like money is going down a sinkhole. Senior management needs to provide adequate, but not excessive resources, as well as give the team the needed authority and autonomy.

This often requires a leap of faith from management. With all the ambiguity involved in both the technology and the market, the only thing a radical project can be certain of is initial failure, and senior management must persevere if the project is ever to succeed. If senior management loses faith in the project, they will cut off funding, and the project will come to naught. Many radical innovation projects are canceled—and should be. When a project is hopeless, senior management must consider calling it quits. Yet without perseverance, without staying the course for the long haul, you cannot create a radical blockbuster. You need to look for the signs from the market and the laboratory that the project will ultimately succeed. Corning received just enough positive feedback that their seemingly wayward journey would ultimately lead to the promised land.

We do not advocate that a radical innovation initiative should have unlimited resources. That may very well detract from the team's effectiveness. We found that when a team is given seemingly inexhaustible resources, the vision of the project is likely to ramp up beyond what's necessary or appropriate. The Lisa team at Apple, housed in luxurious offices with unlimited resources, was unable to restrain itself as their envisioned new computer grew and grew. The vision of their computer went from $2,000 to $10,000. Big difference. Big failure.

But unlike senior management's intimate participation on a traditional NPD, on radical innovation the senior manager—the CEO, COO, or division head—is not likely to be actively involved with the team, but instead supporting it at arm's length. What is the same is that both senior management and team members maintain a crystal-clear understanding of the project's objective, and wholeheartedly believe it can succeed. The final commercial application may shift, the Project Pillars will most likely change as the technology is perfected, and the market target will be refined, but the overarching goal must be shared by all, or the project will die.

What does this mean in terms of dollars and time? Motorola spent fifteen years and $150 million to bring cellular telephones to market. Corning took nearly as much time and approximately $200 million in investment to make optical fibers commercially feasible.

"Every so often, you bet your company on something," said Corning CEO Amory Houghton. And so he did. He continued to fund the project, though for years there seemed to be no profitable end in sight.

Strategic Imperative Fuels Radical Innovation

Unless the opportunity for a radical innovation is strategically central to the business, management will likely fail to muster the staying power to persist during twists, turns, and unpleasant surprises that are to be expected on radical innovation projects. Inevitable setbacks will be interpreted as justification for disengagement rather than as springboards for new efforts. Strategic imperative largely fuels the staying power necessary for a radical innovation. Once again, crisis is a good motivator. During the development of fiber optics in the mid-1970s, Corning was having a difficult time. Its reliance on glass cookware and other conventional products was not enough, and the company was in trouble with thousands laid off. Corning needed a groundbreaking new product. Crisis was the stimulus, and optical fiber was, in the words of Dave Duke, "our kind of business."

VISION

How can you develop a vision for a radically new product? How can you see into your metaphorical crystal ball when it is so cloudy? With incremental innovations, the vision for a new product should answer customer needs and desires, but that can be impossible when you may not even know the category your new product will fit into, or if it will create an entirely new category. With that kind of uncertainty, you probably don't have any idea who your customers will be, or what the market will look like when your new product is ready. As Andy Hertzfeld, one of the Apple employees who worked on the successful Apple II, remarks: "You can't design a revolutionary new product by asking customers what they want—they will always tell you they want ten percent better than what they have. They don't

know the possibilities, and won't be able to imagine the revolutionary product."

Since it is impossible to determine the market—when both the
technology and the market will be evolving together over a period of
years—we puzzled over how companies that developed blockbuster
radical innovations got a feel for the market they would one day be
entering. How could they possibly imagine what the market would
be? Who the competitors would be and what price they should set?
Could they simply offer an unfinished product for sale, and then
produce it after the first orders? While such Gamma testing can be
enormously cost-effective for incrementally new products, it frequently yields erroneous information with radical innovations.

Consider what happened to Corning. The British Post Office
had asked for optical fibers for use in videophones. Corning delivered a product that exceeded their demands, but it was rejected
anyway because the cost to deliver a picture phone was still too
expensive. Conclusion? That no market for optic fibers would exist
until the twenty-first century! At telecommunications and cable
companies around the world, including AT&T, the reaction was
similarly discouraging. Had Corning listened to the market, they
would have abandoned the optical fiber business.[7]

Designer-Inspired Development

Since market reaction is likely to be off the mark because customers
don't know what they don't know, the team must turn inward to create the vision. Designer-inspired development turned up again and
again with radical innovation. The usefulness of the product is
immediately obvious to the designers/engineers, because they are
developing a product for themselves. It's what the Apple folks did

when they designed their newest computers. It's what Kim Edwards insisted on when he tried to install the old storage device (preceding Zip) that Iomega had made hopelessly complicated to install.

Lucy and Maurer and others working in the lab intuitively knew they were creating something that would be useful in long-distance telecommunication. But the impact of having several international corporations and governmental agencies so closely involved helped provide direction. These organizations invested in the venture, and in doing so, effectively became part of the team. They helped refine and validate the Project Pillar of using optical fibers for long-distance communication. However, in looking back we saw that this vision would change several times: from something to be used in picture phones to long-distance telecommunication; then, it was local access networks, or short-distance telecommunications; then it was—no wait—let's go back to long-distance telecommunications. The important point is that the team—both scientists at Corning and the cabling companies—bought into the new vision. Other radically new blockbuster products exhibited a similar pattern and had a series of visions, and Project Pillars, that changed over time as the product was refined. Success demands that the team follow suit and buy into each version of the vision.

So, unlike our previous recommendation that a new product vision be clear and stable at the onset of development, that rule does not apply when creating a radical innovation. Once target goal 20 dB/km was reached in the lab, the vision of how optical fibers might be used was like a moving target. It was flexible and it must be, because what the product will be is unknown as the researchers forge ahead in as yet undiscovered territory. For a while—for quite a while—the ultimate vision will be clouded.

You could compare establishing a vision for such a new product to plotting a course for a ship to reach a new land in dense fog. Everyone agrees when the ship leaves port that they want to get to the new land, and everybody agrees where that new land is. But the fog makes it hard to navigate more than a few feet ahead, so when the ship anchors, the crew learns they are not where they thought they wanted to be. They have to plot a new course and set out again. Both the team on board the ship and senior management financing the voyage must have the same understanding of the goal. Think of Columbus and his crew (Lucy, Maurer, Keck, and Schultz) setting out to discover new lands with Ferdinand and Isabella (Corning's senior management, and later, the outside partners) back home in Spain financing the venture.

PROCESS

As we analyzed how radical innovations were brought to market, we quickly saw that very few of the traditional development phases for incremental innovations applied. Two factors preclude their use in radical innovation.

First, customer concept testing in the traditional sense is all but impossible. How can a potential customer tell you to tweak a new product when the tweaking required is nothing short of a total overhaul?[8] Corning tried to configure fiber optics for picture phones and long-distance telephone lines, but encountered a decidedly cool reception from possible customers for years. After what must have been a frustrating decade-long development process, the long-distance market emerged only with the breakup of AT&T. The picture phone business? Commercially, it's slowly coming out of its cocoon as we write this, nearly three decades after Bell Labs put its picture phone on hold.

Second, during the long lead time required for a radical innovation—usually ten years or more—the market changes. By the time the product is ready, some markets that once seemed like likely targets won't even exist anymore. During this long development period, any number of factors are likely to have changed, including customer preferences, competitive products, environmental regulations, and new safety concerns. A change in any one of them may dramatically alter what the new product can, or should, do.

Given these constraints, companies developing radical innovations usually try several concept-to-market strategies one after another until they find one that works, as did Corning. When one looked like a blind alley, they pursued another. Yes, it's complex. Yes, it's costly. How do companies manage it?

Think of the approach as a series of "experiments," with each archetype yielding more information about the technology and the market. The initial product, or experiment, is not the culmination of the development process, but rather the first step in learning what the product will be.[9] Unlike other innovation, the first models here are probably quite far removed from the final product. Instead of helping the team to configure the final features of the product, as with the SoundStation and Zip Drive, these models help the team locate its market—a big difference from incremental innovation. Over time, and with each successive experiment, the product comes closer to its final form and the market comes into focus. Radical innovations benefit greatly from extensive experimenting through prototyping. (See Figure 9.1.)

Launching Radical Innovations as a Market Test

In radical innovation, the idea of a product launch—the moment the new product becomes a commercial entity—is more of a series

Percentage of Radical Innovation Teams
Proficient at Learning from Prototypes

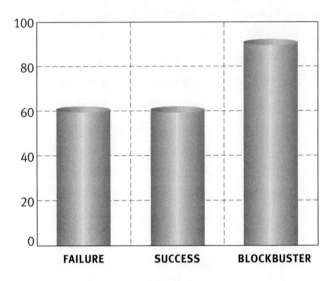

FIGURE 9.1

Blockbuster teams developing radical innovations relied on prototypes. They were one and a half times more likely to excel at learning from prototypes than either failures or successes.

of launches of various prototypes over many years. During the process, the key questions are not, What is the right product? What features do we need? Instead they are: What steps can we take to learn everything we need to know about the product and market? How do we incorporate that information into our product development?

Each new unveiling of a trial product or probe slightly modifies both the product as well as—and this may be surprising—the market for the innovation. So there is neither a conventional launch nor a stable market target. The ultimate target may not be known in the early stages of rolling out one version after another. Just as the vision is a moving target, so does the finish line keep moving. Indeed, one way to view the process for radical innovation is as a vehicle for refining the technology, as well as finding the market.

This "probe-and-learn"[10] process differs from traditional Lickety Stick in several ways. One, the time between prototypes is almost certain to be far longer than for incremental innovation.[11] Two, with incremental innovation, you can throw concepts or sketches against the proverbial wall (the market) and obtain constructive feedback that costs only pennies and can be done early in a program. When Vecta's Bob Beck showed early sketches of the company's ergonomic, stackable chairs to dealers at a trade show, he got valuable feedback that in a sense cost nothing, for the outside designers completed the initial sketches without charge and he would have been at the trade show whether or not he had a new design concept to try out. The dealers instantly understood why it would be a winner. In contrast, showing a sketch and obtaining *accurate* feedback for a radical innovation is probably impossible. You can't realistically ask customers to comment on something that is beyond their comprehension.

We repeat that much of the early testing will go on within the team. As we noted earlier, the teams are most likely to be designing the product for themselves, and consequently, they are the market they are testing. The Motorola cellular phone is a case in point. Listen to Jim Caile, Motorola's head of cell phone marketing, describe the moment he knew the company had a hit on their hands:

We had a test system in Schaumburg [Illinois, site of Motorola's corporate offices] in 1977. I was carrying my portable and was walking across our campus to the Tower [a distant office building] to attend a meeting. My phone rang; it was my secretary informing me that the meeting had been canceled. I didn't have to walk all the way there. At that moment I knew that this was the greatest thing since sliced bread. This was as close to a sure thing as there is.

INFORMATION EXCHANGE

Did teams working on radical innovations exchange knowledge differently from the teams working on incremental innovations? Yes . . . and no. The yes applies to what team members have learned individually and from one another on the team by personal contact, that is, transactive memory. In the beginning, as the team is trying to figure out what their project is, it is difficult to document much that is meaningful. Transactive memory comprises all or nearly all of the knowledge exchange. Instead of weekly or monthly status reports, team members are likely to have daily meetings as they work side-by-side trying to sort this out. No need to bring anybody up-to-date with a status report; everybody is always up-to-date.

Little or No Cross-Team Information Exchange

The big difference in effective learning between incremental and radical teams is what they don't do. They do not learn much from other teams. Since the radical innovation team needs to develop fresh ways of looking for solutions, interacting with other teams, or *cross-team* learning, from teams inside the organization, actually may be detrimental. That's why companies form what are called *skunk works*—autonomous groups with adequate authority and resources—to work on radical innovations, because such teams must be free to break with tradition.* These teams must not be encumbered with corporate axioms such as, "We have always done it that way, and will continue to do it that way." They must be free to try new things.

Cross-team learning hampered Hewlett-Packard's initial attempt in 1989 to compete with a radical innovation in the PC market. HP had a history of developing successful calculators and minicomputers, and the company's first PC came out of their calculator division. On paper, it made perfect sense; in reality, it was something else again. Since the same people who had developed HP's easily transportable—and successful—calculators had designed the PC, they gave it features that their calculators had: they made it both compact and portable. But to meet those Project Pillars, they gave it a five-inch screen, large for a calculator, but way too small for a computer. Both team and senior management failed to realize that what worked in the calculator business did not translate to the PC. Yes, HP's computer was lightweight and compact, but its features severely limited the computer's performance and capabilities.

The product was a dud. HP did not launch a successful PC for another fifteen years. Had HP created a new business unit—a skunk works that freed technical and marketing people from HP traditions—and given them autonomy and authority—the story might have been different. Cross-team learning should play a limited role—or possibly none at all—in radical innovation.

---

* Skunk works are also known by a variety of other names including tiger teams, autonomous work groups, new venture units, self-managed work groups, and experimental departments.

Arrogance Kills Learning

What kills radical innovation? Intellectual arrogance—thinking you know more than you do. Recent Ph.D.s Keck and Schultz benefited from not "knowing" that the goal of 20 dB/km would be "impossible" to attain. At Apple on the failed Lisa team, it was a different story. The best and brightest from a number of different companies were brought together to design the company's new computer. The problem was that they all thought so highly of themselves that they assumed they didn't have to listen to one another. That old adversary—arrogance—threw up a wall of smugness that ruined information exchange within the team.

Such arrogance will destroy any team working on a radical innovation. On a radical project, all must be humble enough to learn from each other, regardless of scholarly degrees and past accomplishments. Of course, it helps if everybody on the team respects each other's ability.

Market Learning

The final type of knowledge exchange is information gained outside the firm, that is, from competitors, suppliers, and customers. With radical innovation, such market learning plays a minor role at the onset. How can you learn from a market that has no concept of the product you are developing? If you had asked executives in 1975 if they thought they would want or need a PC at their desk, nearly everybody would have said no.[12] Listening to the customer would have been useless. It would be like asking a six-year-old what kind of learning tools she would need years hence when she was a graduate student in biochemistry. Think of the child as the current marketplace being asked about inventions yet to be discovered. Neither the child nor the market can predict how each will use the tools of tomorrow.

To sum up the different patterns of learning necessary for radical innovation: teams need (1) excellent transactive memory within a team that encourages a free flow of information; (2) an adequate but not an overreliance on market learning, focusing on competitive technological alternatives; and (3) restricted cross-team learning between teams within the company.

TEAMWORK

While a high degree of collaboration is a hallmark of all blockbuster teams, regardless of the kind of project, it is particularly apparent on NPD teams working on radical innovations. In fact, all the teams we studied who achieved blockbuster success—such as Corning's fiber optics—scored a perfect ten in teamwork. (See Figure 9.2.)

As noted earlier, one of the main factors involved in effective teamwork on any project is that all buy into the Project Pillars. It is no different when working on a radical innovation—all must share a common understanding of the project's goal. What is different on a radical innovation is that the end use of the product may not yet be clear or understood. No one is certain where it will end up, but throughout the process, when the vision is changing, the team must accept each shift and go where it takes them, until it succeeds or the vision shifts again.

With incremental innovations, the team can have a devil's advocate who asks the difficult questions, questions that ultimately help the team do the hard thinking that helps them reach the goal. However, if the team has what we call a hole-poker—someone who

Percentage of Radical Innovation Teams
That Excelled in Teamwork

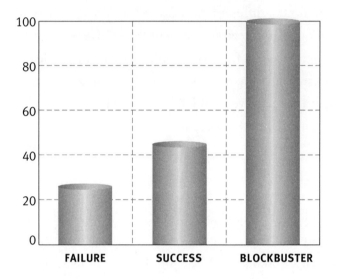

FIGURE 9.2

Blockbuster radical innovation teams all excelled in teamwork, and were more than twice as likely to excel in it than moderately successful teams, and almost four times more likely than failed teams.

finds fault with everything the team is trying to accomplish—the team's chances of success are markedly diminished. With a radical innovation, a hole-poker will certainly have a heyday because there will be ample opportunities to find fault due to the complexity of the project. His influence can severely impede progress and destroy morale. That old saw, one bad apple can spoil the bunch, undeniably applies here.

The team needs people who are positive about the program, who believe that though the goal is unclear and difficult to reach, it is not beyond accomplishing.

Another difference in the teamwork aspect of radical innovation is the size of the team. At the beginning the "team" is likely to consist of only a few people, perhaps even only one, as it did at Corning when Maurer was working alone in his spare time. Here, the technical people will probably drive the program. Later on, as a radical innovation comes closer to its final realization, not only will the number of people in the lab increase, marketing will join the team, and become increasingly important as time passes. Eventually, both marketing and technical professionals will be needed to conduct market probes, or learning experiments. By the time the product finally is launched, marketing will be steering the ship.

ALWAYS A RISKY BUSINESS

Developing and commercializing radical innovations is risky. Obstacles and unexpected challenges crop up everywhere. Senior management will need to budget for the project despite a finish line that keeps moving. Project Pillars will most likely emanate from team members who are also their own customers. The process will consist of probing different markets with different models, but at a slower pace than Lickety Stick for incremental innovations. Information and knowledge will likely be shared extensively within the team, but not absorbed from outside teams. And team members will need to work closely together to pull this off.

Yes, there are many uncertainties. But when you do succeed the payoff can be enormous.

The Message to Management

Breaking Through the Bureaucracy at NASA

A recent study of more than two hundred CEOs of the thousand largest companies in the United States indicated that they believed that new product development was the single most important source of future growth for their companies. The same study also reported that these CEOs spend over twice as much time on financial planning as they do on new product development.[1] But what if you could launch a blockbuster product that significantly improves the bottom line of your company—or one that turns a failing company into a powerhouse in its category, as did many of the blockbusters we've written about?

Think of what happened at Iomega, a company whose bottom line was skidding southward when the Zip Drive was launched—it raised the stock price from $7 a share to an after-stock-split equivalent of $112 a share in *four months* and increased sales from $141 million to $1.2 billion in two years. And Iomega is not alone in attaining the kind of turnaround a blockbuster can produce, as our decade-long research illustrates. This kind of success is within reach, whether your company is a start-up, a small business, a mid-sized company, or a multinational conglomerate.

Throughout the pages of this book, we've shared *what* the five practices of blockbuster teams are, as well as *how* to implement them. We've stressed that it is not enough to excel in one or two of the five practices. To create a blockbuster, it is not sufficient to merely set up clear and stable Project Pillars, for instance, or follow the rapid-prototyping process we call Lickety Stick, or have great teamwork, but with little involvement from senior management. Blockbuster teams must excel *in all five practices,* from concept to launch to refinement. Think of the five practices as links in a chain—if one or two are weak, the chain will likely fail.

Senior management involvement is an integral link in the blockbuster chain. Without it, the chances of failure are great. Especially for nonradical projects, senior management helps to establish the Project Pillars, and impose the hard deadlines we found so necessary for success. Senior management's active participation on the project means that the team will have the resources it needs and decisions can be made quickly. Senior management's involvement also confers an inestimable aura of importance to the project, an aura that translates into enthusiasm and the willingness of individuals to work hard and long to succeed.

All of the practices are critical: active senior-management involvement, adequate Project Pillars, adherence to Lickety Stick, superior knowledge exchange, and effective teamwork. But even when all are in place, we admit, it is not easy to create a blockbuster. Outside factors, such as an unforeseen competitor entering the market, a change in senior management, or a downturn in the economy make it difficult to accurately predict the outcome of any new product development initiative.

Realistically, what are your chances? We can best answer that by referring to our data. We evaluated all the teams in our database on a ten-point scale. Based on our statistical analysis of more than seven hundred teams, we found that if your teams perform all five practices poorly (scoring only ones), their chances of launching a blockbuster is less than 1 percent. If, however, your team scored ten on all five practices, your chances of succeeding are 98 percent and of developing a blockbuster increase to over 70 percent. But not a single one of our blockbuster teams achieved that level of excellence for every practice. This means that even if your team doesn't score tens across the board, you can still achieve block-buster success.

Another way to evaluate your chances is to compare your team's performance with teams in our database that scored fives across the board. They had very little chance of achieving blockbuster suc-cess—less than 5 percent. But if their proficiency in all the practices improved from five to eight, their chances of reaching blockbuster status increased over eight times to more than 40 percent! Doesn't that seem worth the effort? (To learn more about how to measure your team's performance and probability of succeeding, see "Meas-uring Team Performance: A Case Study" in Appendix 1.

GETTING INVOLVED

One message ought to be very clear: senior managers must make it a priority to get involved with new product development. Creating innovative new products should be at the top of your list, not some-thing squeezed in between dealing with human resources or prepar-ing to meet with stockholders. Those are important duties, of course, but without innovative new products, your company will likely not win—it may not even survive—in today's competitive marketplace. New products are the lifeblood of any organization.

You don't, however, have to entirely rewrite your current new product development process. Nor must you change your company's culture, reward incentives, or organizational structure. If your company is anything but a start-up company or a very small firm, you should not implement the five practices across the board on *all* your new product development teams, for that would tax your system too much.

What we suggest is that you apply these practices to one project per division. Have each division manager or vice president select one project to take under his or her wing and shepherd it through development, launch, and further refinement. Have your senior executives spend face-time with the customer at their location, and not just over lunch. In some cases, send team members to spend multiple days at the customer's site. After that, the senior manager must help formulate the Project Pillars; carefully choose team members who have the requisite skills; establish a hard deadline for launch; sell the vision to the team to get buy-in; insist that the team hold weekly meetings at least during the early phase focused on what needs to be done that coming week; and demonstrate an avid interest in the project by attending team meetings, or at the very least, by dropping in once a week to see the team. And lastly, the senior manager must not abandon the team after the product is launched. Colgate-Palmolive's experience with Total—the toothpaste that needed to be repositioned before it was a hit—is a good example. The senior manager should not select another project to oversee *until* the product has been launched, *and* an improved version has been thought through with an accompanying marketing strategy.

PICKING A PROJECT

How do you select which project to shepherd? According to a recent study, product selection is one of the most poorly performed aspects of all new product development.[2] But it need not be rocket science. To select the project, consider the following questions:

1. Which project has the greatest upside potential if it succeeds?

2. In which area is your company most vulnerable to competition?

3. Which products could potentially change the competitive landscape in your market?

4. Which project is at the core of your competency?

5. Which project personally excites you?

The answers should give you a good idea which project to choose. If you don't see a potential blockbuster among your choices—or anything that seems close—we have an alternative suggestion. Simply pick one. If nothing else, working on the project will give you practice overseeing a new product team as a senior adviser, and you'll be more attuned to the kind of customer input that may give you the brainstorm that turns into a blockbuster. Once you start working on a project, do not let other senior managers meddle with your team. They will only confuse the team as to who is really in charge, which will lead to dissension and disorganization.

To get started, figure the schedule backward from a hard deadline, possibly a national or international trade show where you will debut the new product. Choose a deadline that is doable, but one that will be a stretch for the team; we found that a twelve-month deadline works best, unless it is a radical innovation. Stretching to meet the deadline brings out the best in the team. Determine what the team can do in the given time, not what they might be able to do if the time were unlimited.

CORPORATE CULTURE CONSTRAINTS

A question that senior managers often ask is how can they implement the Lickety Stick process in an established corporate culture that appears to be diametrically opposed to it. In this situation, create a skunk works or tiger team and let them know that the old rules don't apply, that they have your permission to operate Lickety Stick. We have one last story to tell, one that illustrates how a very large organization, with thousands of employees and layers of management and lots of red tape, was able to break through their established culture and bureaucracy: NASA's Pathfinder project.

BREAKING THROUGH THE BUREAUCRACY AT NASA

In 1994, NASA's Jet Propulsion Laboratory was asked to develop a vehicle that could land on Mars and send back data about the far-away red planet—not a simple task—especially when NASA announced a new mandate for all projects: everything was to be done faster, better, cheaper. The previous Mars landing, twenty-one years earlier, took six years and cost $3 billion in today's dollars. The new task was to land a vehicle on Mars in half the time and for a fraction of the cost. The project was called Pathfinder.

How did the Pathfinder team do it? First, though all the people assigned to the project were from different functions (telecommunications, propulsion, flight-system engineering, product assurance), they were directly responsible to the Pathfinder project, and not their line area at the Jet Propulsion Laboratory. Second, everyone understood that knowledge exchange was critical to their success. Managers kept everybody in the loop on all decisions, which encouraged open communication among all team members, up and down the chain of command. Minimal attention was paid to rank. The team had weekly status reports, informal meetings, and internal peer reviews, allowing for plenty of feedback as they learned what they needed to know together. Third, the managers of the project trusted the expertise of their engineers—even if they didn't understand the technical aspects of the project themselves. As Donna Shirley, project manager for the unmanned vehicle that would actually roam Mars, put it:

> When you are managing really brilliant people, at some point you find it is almost impossible to command or control them because you can't always understand what they are doing. Once they've gone beyond your ability to understand them, then you have to make a choice as a manager. You can limit them—and the project—by your limited expertise, or you can trust them and use your management skills to keep them focused on the goal.

Shirley's trust helped cement their commitment to the mission. This was essential because the workers were putting in incredibly long hours—just as they saw her do. Throughout the project, the team had a very specific goal and deadline, and, as a cost-saving measure, was somewhat understaffed. Launch had to be within a thirty-day window—due to the favorable alignment of the planets— and if they missed it, they would not get the same opportunity for another two years. Missing the deadline became unthinkable.

They had few rules, and they improvised as needed, just like we saw on blockbuster teams in the commercial sector. Risk-taking was encouraged. Failures were seen as an opportunity to learn. And because all four hundred people on the project were at the same site, those who needed to meet in person were able to do so easily.

Not only did the rocket reach Mars after a 300-million-mile trip that took seven months, it successfully landed its package, the six-wheel vehicle called *Sojourner*. The solar batteries that propelled *Sojourner* operated for three full months, two months longer than expected. *Sojourner* roamed the planet and sent back data on the atmosphere and surface properties, as well as sharp pictures of Mars' barren surface. The team had far exceeded the project's goals, and developed some remarkable new technology for space exploration as well. NASA officials were thrilled.

If this kind of can-do culture can be implemented at NASA, it can be done at your company, big or small. But you must be resolute, you must be willing to try something new, you must be able to convince the team they can do it, and you must step up at the onset of the project and stay involved throughout. No "hit-and-run" management, no disappearing into the corner office emerging only when the project runs into trouble, no quick fixes to underlying problems, and no changing the objectives of the project midstream.

A PLAN FOR YOUR TEAM

Changing focus from you to the team for a moment, here's what the team you select needs to do: To begin with, people from both marketing and R&D should visit a range of customers at their place of business to learn what their problems are and how they use current products—both yours and the competition's. If at all possible, marketing and R&D should make the trip together to facilitate communication between the two functions. While there, your team should identify which customers would be willing to evaluate a prototype.

You and your team should then establish Project Pillars and a "hard" launch date. Then get everyone to buy into them. After that, you are ready to build a prototype. It need not be perfect, just good enough that the company is not embarrassed when you show it to potential customers.

WE DON'T PROMISE THE MOON

We do not claim that incorporating the five practices will guarantee blockbuster-off-the-chart success, but without them, you significantly decrease your chances of succeeding. Without implementing the five practices on your next new product development, we can virtually guarantee that you won't have a blockbuster to celebrate two years from now. So, once you've decided to go ahead, give the practices your full attention and enthusiasm. Don't do them halfway. Don't let your teams do them halfway either. Throw yourself into the project one hundred percent, and others will follow your lead.

We don't promise that the project will be a smooth ride—even in the calmest of business environments, you will hit some bumps and potholes that send you back to the drawing board. Yes, it takes a lot of work. Yes, it is risky. Yes, it is stressful. But what are your alternatives? To continue business as usual? To watch the competition come out with the next blockbuster product in your category and wonder how *they* did it? You are your company's visionary. Your new products are the perfect battleground to test and perfect that ability. We've shown you the *what* and the *how*.

The rest is up to you.

MEASURING TEAM PERFORMANCE:
A CASE STUDY

Several years ago, a senior executive from a Fortune 100 company told us she was frustrated with her company's new product teams. The company wanted to improve its new product performance, but senior management needed specifics to give the team—exactly how could they improve? To address this, we developed a benchmarking tool for new product teams to assess their proficiency with the five practices. This allows teams, divisions, and even entire companies, to estimate their probability of success and see which areas need improvement. Teams can clearly and plainly assess how they stack up against other teams in their industry, or against best-in-breed/blockbuster teams from different industries. We call this assessment an Innovation Report Card.

Here's how it works: The project leader and/or two other members of the team complete an innovation audit that has ninety-two items. With that information, we assess how well the team is implementing each of the five practices. Using our database (which now includes nearly 800 teams) from a wide variety of industries, we compare the team with others within its specific industry or with best-in-class teams. Wherever we see that the team is deficient in one of the practices, we conduct one-half-day training sessions designed to address the specific area needing improvement. The best way to explain how it works is to take you through the process with a different company, a mid-sized, consumer-products company that asked us to assess their new product development and commercialization process in two of its divisions. Altogether, we analyzed six projects— three in each division. Project leaders first completed the innovation audit, augmented with phone interviews with the project leaders and team members.

To make our results easier to understand, we assign grades to indicate how each team was performing each practice. Teams receiving a score in the top 10 percent got an A, and teams scoring above the 70th but below the 90th percentile received a B, and so on (see Figure A.1).

Innovation Report Card Grading Curve

GRADE	REFERENCE PERCENTILE RANGE
A	90th percentile and above
B	Above 70th but below 90th percentile
C	Above 30th but below 70th percentile
D	Above 10th but below 30th percentile
F	10th percentile and below

FIGURE A.1

From the information in the audits, we created individual Report Cards for all the projects and summary Report Cards for each division. The division summary Report Cards are shown in Figure A.2.

Division 1 was not very successful. Its projects were failing and it had two major problems: Project Pillars and collaboration. Collaboration suffered considerably due to a lack of team stability. People were prematurely being transferred from one project to another— one manager reported having to finish seventy projects he did not initiate! As a result of this turnover, team members were constantly trying to get to know one another and figure out how to work together, rather than moving forward on the job at hand.

Summary Report Card
Division #1

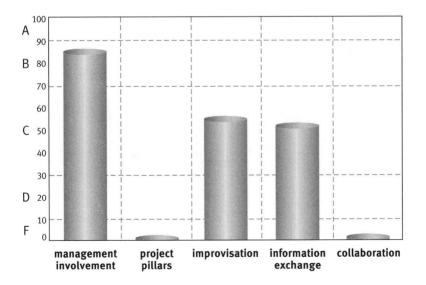

FIGURE A.2

Team instability led to a second problem. With the many changes in the makeup of the team, it was nearly impossible to have stable Pillars, because so many on the team had not been around long enough to buy into them. The information exchange process was mediocre, which compounded the problem, and new team members were not brought up to speed effectively. The net result was a division in deep trouble.

Division 2 was better but still scored straight Cs, reflecting the mediocre success of its new product initiatives. However, Division 2 did have one relatively successful project that excelled in several practices, falling short only in information exchange. For two of the projects, information exchange was graded D. Our audit uncovered

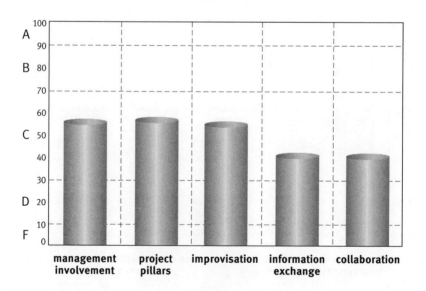

Summary Report Card
Division #2

FIGURE A.3

a lack of effective communication and record keeping. One project manager reported receiving over two hundred faxes every day, and said that many were misfiled or lost.

The results we presented to the CEO were eye-opening. The innovation audits allowed us to highlight strengths and challenges facing his organization in a way that was both specific and quantifiable. Although a couple teams excelled in some selected practices, the general picture was of an organization that had to change quickly to survive. The challenges facing Division 1 were too great and this division was sold entirely. For Division 2, we made a series of recommendations followed by some training that concentrated on clarifying the Pillars before beginning a project (these were incremental innovations, not radical products), establishing better procedures for motivating and retaining its people and creating a more effective system for communicating within its teams and within the company.

After our feedback and training the CEO implemented the following changes:

1. Re-created its entire company mission statement as a first step in providing a clear vision.

2. Made better use of cross-team learning to take advantage of what some teams did well (e.g., information exchange).

3. Created specific objectives to improve its process, which included setting hard deadlines.

4. Analyzed how it was hiring, compensating, and rewarding employees in an effort to improve employee retention and improve team stability.

THE BOTTOM LINE

Although it is difficult to precisely determine how much the innovation audit, and our recommendations and training helped this company, twelve months after implementing the above actions, the following results were obtained for this division:

- Gross margin improved 54 percent.

- Employee retention went up 50 percent.

- Re-works decreased 25 percent.

- Time to market improved 15 percent.

- Customer satisfaction improved 15 percent.

Over the years, we have worked with hundreds of companies. In the beginning, it was surprising to us (and to many of the companies who received them) how well the Innovation Report Card and follow-up training works. The Report Card allows teams and companies to quickly and precisely see how their teams are performing, where they are excelling, where they need improving and their probability of succeeding. Over the last three years, we also observed that different divisions within a company operate differently in how they develop and commercialize new products. Even companies that have a well-documented, rigorous new product process in place may find that one or more divisions are not implementing them by the book. This creates an opportunity to identify practices within a division that can be improved, and for one division to learn from another.

Of course, improvements in your division may not always be as spectacular as they were for the company highlighted. This company had some serious problems, and had considerable room to improve. But, even if only one major problem is uncovered, it can make a big difference in your ability to innovate quickly and effectively.

To obtain a copy of the innovation audit or learn more about the Report Card, send an email to: tips@blockbusterinnovation.com.

INDUSTRIES AND COMPANIES WHO PARTICIPATED IN THIS RESEARCH

Over the past ten years, a wide variety of companies and teams within those companies have participated in this research. These companies represented a range of industries including chemicals, electronics, food, materials, medical and scientific instruments, petroleum, pharmaceuticals, power generation, software, telecommunications, defense, and financial services to name a few. Companies represented small start-ups with a handful of employees to behemoths with thousands of employees like IBM, GE, and the Department of Defense. Our goal was to sample from a diverse cross section of products and industries so that our conclusions could be generalized—not just for one industry or one type of innovation (incremental or radical).

New product development is arguably one of the most proprietary aspects of a company. Some companies that participated in this research preferred to remain anonymous, and we abide by their request. A sample of the other companies that participated includes: 3Com/U.S. Robotics, Air Cruisers, Alliant Precision Fuze Company,

Allied Signal/Honeywell, American Express, Apple, AT&T, Aztec Technology Partners, Becton Dickinson, Bell Atlantic, Bellcore/ Telcordia, Benet Labs, Bestfoods, Blueflame, Booz, Allen and Hamilton, Carrier, Ciba-Gigy, Cisco Systems, Colgate, Corning, CR Bard, Datascope, Delta Airlines, Dialogic/Intel, Digital/Compaq, Exxon, GE, GEC Marconi, Gillette, Handspring, Hartz Mountain, Hewlett-Packard, Hitachi, IBM, International Flavor, Iomega, L3 Communications, Lucent, Merck, Merrill Lynch, MITRE, Monsanto, Motorola, Multi-Arc, Nabisco, NOVARTIS, NYCE, Ogden Energy, Ortho-Clinical Diagnostics/Johnson & Johnson, Pershing, Pilot Technologies, Planters, Primex Technologies, Polycom, Price-WaterhouseCoopers, PSE&G, Quest Diagnostics, Sigma-Netics, Sonus Networks, WorkTools, Verizon, York International, NASA, the U.S. Department of Defense, and the U.S. Department of Commerce.

Some of the blockbuster products that we studied included the following: Apple IIe, Black & Decker Dustbuster, Black & Decker PowerShot stapler, Colgate Total toothpaste, Corning optic fibers, General Electric CAT scanner, Gillette Sensor razor, Handspring Visor, IBM PC, Iomega Zip Drive, Johnson and Johnson/Ortho Diagnostics Koagulab (an instrument for measuring the clotting factor of blood), Kodak FunSaver camera, Lucent (now Aastra) WaveStar Digital Video Systems, a product for high-definition TV broadcasting, Marvin Double-Hung windows, Motorola StarTAC cellular phone, Nova Cruz Xootr scooter, Palm Pilot, Polycom SoundStation, Sequoia Pacific Automatic Voting Machine, Vecta Nesting Kart chairs.

TEST YOUR KNOWLEDGE

Imagine you are vice president of marketing or R&D for a computer component manufacturing company. Your sales total $500 million per year. Your main business is CD ROM read-write drives that you sell exclusively to OEMs. Some of your customers include IBM, HP, and Apple, who install your drives in their computers. You have tried several times in the past to sell directly to end consumers but things did not work out.

Three weeks ago, one of your bright fast-track engineers came to you with a prototype of a new product—a brain-wave activated mouse. It needs no wires and is controlled totally from the user's own brain waves. The engineer built a prototype, but it is only 65 percent accurate. The engineer who had this idea has a history of coming up with innovative solutions that have made your company money, but a few times his ideas did not work out.

What should you do?

BLOCKBUSTER PRACTICE #1: SHOULD YOU . . .

a. Try to keep management at a safe distance until you have the details worked out.

b. Seek a "champion" for the project.

c. Convince a division manager or above to become an active participant in the development team.

d. Provide a small budget to help the researcher more fully develop the prototype.

BLOCKBUSTER PRACTICE #2: SHOULD YOU . . .

a. Conduct a focus group with a cross section of computer users.

b. Hire a market research firm to explore the merits of the idea.

c. Try to get a "user" of this device to join the team—for example, a severely disabled person or a physician who works with the disabled.

d. Formulate Project Pillars now before the project wanders too far off base.

BLOCKBUSTER PRACTICE #3: SHOULD YOU . . .

a. Try to improve the accuracy to an acceptable level before showing it to potential customers.

b. Test the prototype as-is in the marketplace.

c. Show the prototype to the division manager or CEO to find out his/her opinion.

d. Allow the engineer to keep tinkering with it until you have a viable product and an appropriate application.

BLOCKBUSTER PRACTICE #4: SHOULD YOU . . .

a. Document information gained by team members.

b. Develop transactive and mechanistic systems to capture team knowledge.

c. Create a knowledge depository for information obtained on this project.

d. Create a Web site for the project.

BLOCKBUSTER PRACTICE #5: SHOULD YOU . . .

a. Get the best and the brightest people you can find on the team.

b. Try to get people who have worked successfully before on another team to join you—even if it means working on it in their spare time for a while.

c. Form a team and together create the Project Pillars.

d. Hire a consultant to train the team in effective teamwork.

NOTES

PREFACE

1. Greg Stevens, James Burley, and Richard Divine, "Creativity + Business Discipline = Higher Profits Faster from New Product Development," *Journal of Product Innovation Management* 16, no. 5 (1999) pp. 455–468.

2. See Kevin Clancy and Robert Shulman, *The Marketing Revolution: A Radical Manifesto for Dominating the Marketplace* (New York: Harper Business, 1991), p. 6; Robert G. Cooper, 1982 "New Product Success in Industrial Firms," in *Industrial Marketing Management* vol. II (1982) pp. 215–223; and Gary Strauss, "Building on Brand Names: Companies Freshen Old Product Lines," *USA Today*, March 20, 1992, pp. B1, B2.

3. See Philip Kotler and Gary Armstrong, *Principles of Marketing*, 5th ed. (Englewood Cliffs, N.J.: Prentice-Hall, 1994). Gary S. Lynn, Joseph G. Morone, and Albert S. Paulson, "Marketing and Discontinuous Innovation: The Probe and Learn Process," *California Management Review* 38, no. 3 (Spring 1996). Joseph G. Morone, *Winning in High Tech Markets* (Boston: Harvard Business School Press, 1993). Christopher Power, "Flops," *Business-Week*, August 16, 1993, pp. 76–82; and G. L. Urban and J. R. Hauser, *Design and Marketing of New Products*, 2nd ed. (Englewood Cliffs, N.J.: Prentice-Hall, 1993).

1: HOW BLOCKBUSTERS HAPPEN

1. Robert C. Camp, *Benchmarking: The Search for Industry Best Practices that Lead to Superior Performance* (Milwaukee, WI: Quality Press, 1989), p. 10.

2. James H. Harrington and James S. Harrington, *High Performance Benchmarking* (New York: McGraw-Hill, 1996), p. 12.

3. Ibid.

4. Bureau of Business Practice, *Benchmarking: Action Plans and Legal Issues* (Waterford, CT: 1994).

5. Robert C. Camp et al., *Global Cases in Benchmarking: Best Practices from Organizations Around the World* (Milwaukee, WI: ASQ Quality Press, 1998).

6. For references on teams, see John Katzenbach and Douglas Smith, *The Wisdom of Teams* (New York: HarperBusiness, 1993); on the new product development process, see Robert Cooper, *Winning at New Products,* 3rd ed. (Cambridge, MA: Perseus Publishing, 2001), C. Merle Crawford and C. Anthony DiBenedetto, *New Products Management,* 6th ed. (Boston: Irwin McGraw-Hill, 2000), and Steven Wheelwright and Kim Clark, *Revolutionizing Product Development* (New York: The Free Press, 1992); on marketing, see Edward McQuarrie, *Customer Visits,* 2nd ed. (Thousand Oaks, CA: Sage Publications, 1998), Geoffrey Moore, *Inside the Tornado* (New York: Harper-Collins, 1999), and Jakki Moore, *Marketing of High-Technology Products and Innovation* (Upper Saddle River, N.J.: Prentice-Hall, 2001); on prototyping, see Michael Schrage, *Serious Play* (Boston: Harvard Business School Press, 2000); and on radical innovation or disruptive technologies, see Clayton Christensen, *The Innovator's Dilemma* (Boston: Harvard Business School Press, 1997) and Richard Leifer et al., *Radical Innovation* (Boston: Harvard Business School Press, 2000).

2: THE FIVE CRITICAL PRACTICES AT WORK

1. Kelly Spang, "Iomega Shipping ATAPI Interface Zip Drive," *Computer Reseller News,* March 24, 1997, pp. 73–74.

2. Internal Iomega Company video on the Zip history.

3. Ibid.

4. Ibid.

5. Ibid.

6. Ibid.

3: THE BUCK STARTS HERE

1. Others have suggested that a "hands-on champion" is critical for success when the project represents a substantial cost or represents a strategic redirection, which was true for many of the blockbuster projects that we studied. See Diana Day, "Raising Radicals: Different Processes for Championing Innovative Corporate Ventures," *Organization Science* 5, no. 2 (1994): 149–172, and Richard Leifer et al., *Radical Innovation* (Boston: Harvard Business School Press, 2000).

2. Tara Parker-Pope, "Colgate Places a Huge Bet on a Germ-Fighter," *Wall Street Journal*, December 29, 1997, p. B1.

3. Christine Bittar, "Jack Haber: Getting Totaled," *Brandweek*, October 12, 1998, pp. S34–S38.

4. Bette Popovich, "Oral Hygiene Receives Total Support," *Chemical Market Reporter*, May 11, 1998, pp. FR18–FR20.

5. Our conclusions have similarities to that of others writing in the field, who have suggested that senior managers can and should exert "subtle control" over a project. That is, the senior managers develop and communicate a distinctive, coherent product concept, and delegate authority to project teams so that they have enough autonomy to be motivated and creative. See Shona L. Brown and Kathleen M. Eisenhardt, "Product Development: Past Research, Present Findings, and Future Directions," *Academy of Management Review* (Mississippi State) 20 (April 1995): 343–378. Also, the concept of an executive sponsor is discussed in Steven C. Wheelwright and Kim B. Clark, *Revolutionizing Product Development* (New York: The Free Press, 1992).

6. R. Waine Boss, "Is the Leader Really Necessary? The Longitudinal Results of Leader Absence in Team Building," *Public Administration Quarterly* 23, no. 4 (Winter 2000): 471–486.

7. Rajesh Sethi, Daniel C. Smith, and C. Whan Park, "Cross-Functional Product Development Teams, Creativity, and the Innovativeness of New Consumer Products," *Journal of Marketing Research* (Chicago), February 2001.

4: CLEAR AND STABLE VISION (PART 1)

1. Project Pillars differ from a Product Innovation Charter because the latter generally pertains to a broad opportunity not to a specific product that a group has yet to create. For more information on Product Innovation Charters, see C. Merle Crawford and C. Anthony DiBenedetto, *New Products Management*, 6th ed. (Boston: Irwin McGraw-Hill, 2000), pp. 50–58.

2. Donald Reinertsen, the originator of the term, "fuzzy front-end," personal conversation.

3. Particular thanks to Gina Colarelli O'Connor of Rensselaer Polytechnic Institute for helping us to develop these questions.

4. The period of ferment, also called the "era of ferment" or "prepara-digmatic design phase," is when many product varieties and variations vie for customer acceptance and competitors aggressively fight over the new versus existing technology, e.g., vacuum tubes versus semiconductors. For a more detailed discussion of this concept, see P. Anderson and M. Tushman, "Technological Discontinuities and Dominant Designs: A Cyclical Model of Technological Change," *Administrative Science Quarterly* 35 (1990): 604–633.

5. Eric von Hippel, *The Sources of Innovation* (New York: Oxford University Press (1988).

5: CLEAR AND STABLE VISION (PART 2)

1. Eric von Hippel, *The Sources of Innovation* (New York: Oxford University Press, 1988).

2. These questions were adapted from Edward McQuarrie, *Customer Visits*, 2nd ed. (Thousand Oaks, CA: Sage Publications, 1998), p. 53.

3. See Robert Cooper, *Winning at New Products*, 3rd ed. (Cambridge, MA: Perseus Publishing, 2001).

6: LICKETY STICK IMPROVISATION

1. "A Decade of Design: Gold: Sharpshooter," *BusinessWeek*, November 29, 1999.

2. For more discussion on rapid iteration of prototypes, see Michael Schrage, *Serious Play* (Boston: Harvard Business School Press, 2000).

3. C. Merle Crawford and C. Anthony DiBenedetto, *New Products Management*, 6th ed. (Boston: Irwin McGraw-Hill, 2000), pp. 338–339.

4. See Schrage, *Serious Play*. The use of successive prototypes is also described in R. S. Rosenbloom and M. A. Cusumano, "Technical Pioneering and Competitive Advantage: The Birth of the VCR Industry," *California Management Review* 29, no. 4 (1987): 51–76 and Cooper, *Winning at New Products* (2001) notes that 50 percent of the failed products that he studied did not test prototype with their customers; and Marco Iansiti, "Shooting the Rapids," *California Management Review* 38, no. 1 (Fall 1995): 37–58.

5. For more information on virtual prototypes, see Ely Dahan and V. Srinivasan, "The Predictive Power of Internet-Based Product Concept Testing Using Visual Depiction and Animation" (working paper, Stanford Business School, 2000).

6. Quoted in Schrage, *Serious Play*, pp. 164–165.

7: INFORMATION EXCHANGE

1. Gregg Williams and Rob Moore, "The Apple Story: Part I, Early History," *Byte*, December 1984.

2. Guy Kawasaki, *Selling the Dream* (New York: HarperCollins, 1991).

3. Ibid.

4. See Apple Computer, Inc., "Corporate Timeline," January 1993; and Michael Moritz, *The Little Kingdom* (New York: William Morrow, 1984), p. 323.

5. "Apple Computer's Counterattack Against IBM," *Business-Week*, January 16, 1984, p. 78.

6. GUI had been developed at PARC, but was not successfully commercialized.

7. D. M. Wegner, "Transactive Memory: A Contemporary Analysis of Group Mind," in B. Mullen and G. R. Geeithals, eds., *Theories of Group Behavior* (New York: Springer-Verlag, 1986).

8. D. W. Liang, R. L. Moreland, and L. Argote, "Group Versus Individual Training and Group Performance: The Mediating Role of Transactive Memory," *Personality and Social Psychology Bulletin* 21 (1995): 384–393.

9. Edward McQuarrie, *Customer Visits*, 2nd ed. (Thousand Oaks, CA: Sage Publications, 1998).

8: COLLABORATION UNDER PRESSURE

1. Pat Dillon, "The Next Small Thing," *Fast Company*, June 1998.

2. Ibid.

3. The regression model yielded an overall multiple correlation of R = .65, which was significant beyond the .001 level. Coefficients shown are standardized. All of the regression coefficients were statistically significant at the .001 level.

4. Connie J. G. Gersick, "Time and Transition in Work Teams: Toward a New Model of Group Development, *Academy of Management Journal* (Mississippi State) 31 (March 1988): 9–41.

5. Ibid.

6. Geoffrey C. Ward and Ken Burns, *Baseball: An Illustrated History* (New York: Knopf, 1994).

7. Other research has shown that the more confidence that the team has in their ability to succeed the more likely it is that they will succeed. This belief has been called *collective efficacy*. See Albert Bandura, *Self-Efficacy: The Exercise of Control* (New York: W. H. Freeman, 1997), p. 469.

8. Kenneth R. Thompson, Wayne A. Hochwarter, and Nicholas J. Mathys, "Stretch Targets: What Makes Them Effective?" *Academy of Management Executive* 11, no. 3 (1997): 48–60.

9. Preston Smith and Donald Reinertsen, *Developing Products in Half the Time* (New York: Van Nostrand Reinhold, 1995), p. 119.

10. Source: B. J. Avolio, J. M. Howell, and J. J. Sosik, "A Funny Thing Happened on the Way to the Bottom Line: Humor as a Moderator of Leadership Style Effects," *Academy of Management Journal* 42 (1999): 219–227.

9: WHAT ABOUT RADICAL INNOVATION?

1. Ira C. Magaziner and Mark Patinkin, *The Silent War: Inside the Global Business Battles Shaping America's Future* (New York: Random House, 1989), pp. 274–275.

2. The joint venture partners included Pirelli in Italy, Siemens in Germany, BICC in Britain, CGE in France, and Furukawa in Japan, as well as governmental technical agencies, CNET in France, and CSELT in Italy. They all invested money to keep the project alive.

3. Joseph Morone, *Winning in High-Tech Markets* (Boston: Harvard Business School Press, 1993), p. 149.

4. Interview with Thomas MacAvoy by Joseph Morone (March 22, 1991).

5. Interview with William Armistead by Joseph Morone (April 1991).

6. Michael E. Porter, *Cases in Competitive Strategy* (New York: Free Press, 1983), p. 340.

7. The challenge of listening to existing customers for radical innovations or disruptive technologies are discussed in Clayton Christensen, *The Innovator's Dilemma* (Boston: Harvard Business School Press, 1997).

8. Ibid.

9. Gary Lynn, Joe Morone, and Albert Paulson, "Marketing Discontinuous Innovation: The Probe and Learn Process," *California Management Review* 38, no. 3 (Spring 1996): 8–37.

10. Ibid.

11. Richard Leifer et al., *Radical Innovation* (Boston: Harvard Business School Press, 2000). The authors describe a series of what they term revolutionary innovations, having found that the mean time between prototypes was not significant for these types of innovations but it was significant for evolutionary projects.

12. See Christensen, *The Innovator's Dilemma.*

10: THE MESSAGE TO MANAGEMENT

1. Richard Hise and Stephen McDaniel, "From American Competitiveness and the CEO: Who's Minding the Shop," *Sloan Management Review,* Winter 1988, p. 52.

2. Robert Cooper, *Winning at New Products,* 3rd ed. (Cambridge, MA: Perseus Publishing, 2001), p. 215.

INDEX

Page numbers in *italics* refer to captions.

DATE DUE
